GET STARTED
IN WRITING AN
ILLUSTRATED
CHILDREN'S
BOOK

Teach®
Yourself

Get Started in Writing an Illustrated Children's Book

Lucy Courtenay

Paperback ISBN: 978 1 473 61184 9

eBook ISBN: 978 1 473 61185 6

1

Typeset by Cenveo® Publisher Services.

Printed and bound in Great Britain by CPI Group (UK) Ltd., Croydon, CR0 4YY.

John Murray Learning policy is to use papers that are natural, renewable and recyclable products and made from wood grown in sustainable forests. The logging and manufacturing processes are expected to conform to the environmental regulations of the country of origin.

John Murray Learning
Carmelite House
50 Victoria Embankment
London EC4Y 0DZ
www.hodder.co.uk

To family and friends and strangers who endured the refrain 'I want to write children's books' for the full 13 years that it took.
Thank you.

Contents

About the author

Lucy Courtenay has been officially writing children's books since 1999, and unofficially for a lot longer than that. She has written over a hundred books, including titles for series such as Animal Ark and Beast Quest, covering books for every age range from first readers to teenage, and every extent from 17 words to 70,000. She is proud to lurk beneath 13 pseudonyms to date, including Enid Blyton. Among her latest books is young adult romantic comedy *The Kiss*, published by Hodder Children's Books under her own name. The next title for Hodder Hodder Children's Books will be *Movie Night*, publishing in January 2017. She is an industry editor for Cornerstones Literary Consultancy and is also a freelance editor of children's fiction.

Acknowledgements

Special thanks to all those authors and illustrators I cornered at parties to ask their opinion – particularly Peter Bently, Alex T. Smith, Liz Pichon, Lauren Child, Ben Cort, Chris Riddell and Julia Donaldson.

Introduction

'A parent saw a child drawing a horse, and it was purple. The
parent asked the child, "Why are you drawing a purple horse?
I've never seen purple horses." To which the child replied,
"How sad for you."'

Anonymous

Can you picture a purple horse? If you are still in touch with the
child that you once were, then you should be able to summon
one to mind without too much difficulty. If you can't – if
childhood feels too long ago, too fuzzy, not much missed – don't
despair. This book is here to help you find your way back to a
place where life was simple yet wonderfully mysterious at the
same time.

Children see things differently from adults. They have less
knowledge on which to draw, by which to make comparisons,
through which to understand the world. They make sense of life
via their own experience. They know the colour purple. They
recognize a horse. Their logic leads them to conclude that a
purple horse is an interesting possibility, worth exploring with
a felt-tip pen. To write successfully for children, you need to be
open to seeing the world afresh in this way, as you did when
you were a child yourself. Once you have mastered this, the
possibilities are wide-ranging.

This is a book primarily aimed at writers. As a writer myself,
I feel qualified to talk about the words, but cautious about
offering detailed advice on how to illustrate. There is plenty
of relevant information in here for illustrators, and I hope at
least to illuminate some of the darker corners of that aspect of
publishing, but the focus will be very much on how to write
with illustrations in mind, and not the other way around. The
most valuable piece of advice for illustrators that I will offer
here is that, while you are always welcome to develop and
include illustrations in any writing that you submit to publishers,
ninety-nine times out of a hundred your images will be redrawn.

Because here is the paradox. While the perfect illustrated book must work as a whole and indivisible thing, words and pictures are entirely separate components during the publishing process itself. There are separate contracts and separate schedules, separate representative agents and separate financial arrangements. Your pictures will not be the deciding factor in whether or not a publisher takes your writing. If you take away nothing else from this book, do your very best to take away this.

By their nature, illustrated books are generally aimed at younger readers, from babies to around ten years old. There are exceptions, of course. Patrick Ness's *A Monster Calls*, a hard-hitting book for teen readers about cancer and loss based on an idea by the late Siobhan O'Dowd and illustrated by Jim Kay, made history in 2012 by being the first book ever to win both the Carnegie Medal for children's fiction and the Kate Greenaway Medal for children's illustration. But the rarity of such an event proves how different the two fields generally are. There is also a vast canon of graphic novels and comics for older readers that I won't touch on here. For the purposes of this book, we will be focusing on the younger end of the market. In particular, we will look at the interdependence of words and pictures for younger readers, and how to use that extra dimension to make your stories sing.

We won't start *too* young, however. Publishers generally produce books for nought to two-year-olds themselves, using in-house editors to write the few words needed. Often going by the term 'novelty books', material for this age range includes alphabet and counting books, board and buggy and bath books, touch-and-feel, lift-the-flap, scratch-and-sniff, colouring and pop-up books, to give a few examples. There is no opportunity for a first-time writer to cut their teeth on books like these. If it makes you feel better, there isn't much opportunity for experienced writers either. So if you have a wonderful idea for children aged between nought and two, I'm afraid I would advise you to shelve it. But don't lose heart. There are lots of opportunities out there to write for children aged three and older that we can explore together.

Three- to seven-year-olds love picture books enhanced by a few well-chosen words. Books for this age range are perhaps the books that you think of when you think of children's books: large format, full-colour illustrations, shiny cover and an extent of around 32 pages. Early readers between the ages of five and eight are getting more adventurous, but find pages of unbroken text off-putting and need pictures to comfort and explain as they progress along the great highway towards full literacy. Even fully fledged readers from eight onwards appreciate a little illustration to propel them along, to open windows on a plotline and lend a story a few more angles. As the only illustration in the original editions, I pored over the Hogwarts crest at the start of the original-edition Harry Potter books, translated the motto, used it as a key to unlock a fresh dimension to the story – and I was somewhat older than the intended audience.

Which area is for you? Are you a rare breed like Oliver Jeffers, a writer/illustrator who shot to the top of the 'slush pile' – that toppling heap of unsolicited manuscripts that all too often sit unconsidered beneath an editor's desk – with his picture book *How to Catch a Star*, to win prizes and accolades all over the world? Is rhyme your thing, or comedy, or drama? There are exercises and workshops scattered through this book to help you find out, plus interviews and quotes and glimpses into the lives of writers and other established professionals in the field of children's publishing that will answer questions for you that you may not have known you wanted to ask. This book is your chance to try all these different categories of illustrated children's books on for size, see how they sit alongside your own writing ambitions, and get a feel for the kind of writer that you would like to be.

The approach required in writing non-fiction for children is very different, and I am not best qualified to advise you on it. So we shall be sticking to storytelling, because at least I know where the quicksands are and can show you how to avoid them.

I wish I could tell you that reading this book will guarantee you success in your bid to get published. Sadly, I can't. Many people argue that talent can't be taught, no matter how much exercise and daily practice you throw at it. While it's true that you can't create talent, you *can* improve on whatever talent you possess. Creating children's stories is a craft. It's like pottery but not as messy, or like painting but marginally less colourful. With practice, you can improve. You may not become the next Clarice Cliff through your pottery class, but your pots might stand up where before they flopped sadly to one side. The chances of being the next Pablo Picasso aren't enhanced by attending art classes, but you're more likely, through practice, to produce something that you'd be happy to frame and hang in your own kitchen. If you read this book and follow the exercises and practise every day, then, logically, you will be a better writer than you were when you started. And isn't that why you picked up this book in the first place?

Too often, children's authors suffer the indignity of being asked when they are going to write proper books. Children's books *are* proper books, and they deserve proper attention. Children might be different from adults, but they are not stupid. Remember how it took a child to unmask the idiocy of the Emperor and his court in Hans Christian Andersen's 'The Emperor's New Clothes'? Children know when a book is good, and they will tell you when a book is bad. Their favourites will be read and read again until they fall apart and have to be stuck back together with glue and staples. It's a marvellous fate for a book, and something to aspire to.

I hope that you will be surprised, informed and encouraged by what you discover in these pages as I attempt to guide you through your own adventure. The purple horses are just over the horizon. Let's go round 'em up.

Icons used in this book

- Write – exercises where you'll be asked to create your own piece of writing
- Snapshot – shorter exercises or questions to help you consider a particular aspect of writing illustrated children's books
- Workshop – longer exercises to help you reflect on a piece of writing
- Edit – a chance for you to rework and strengthen a piece you've already created
- Key quote – words of wisdom from those who know
- Key idea – an essential concept to grasp
- Focus point – advice to take forward

Workshop: Before you begin…

It is very important, when you start your journey to become a writer, to get into the habit of always having the right tools to hand. Ideas have a way of sliding in and out of our heads, and it's vital to jot them down as soon as you can. All professional writers have their own way of capturing ideas. I would recommend keeping the following with you at all times:

- notebook / computer tablet – whichever you feel most comfortable using
- pens / pencils / writing implements of choice
- a camera.

Other useful items to be kept at home:

- box files for clippings and photographs
- index cards for sorting your ideas into themes, genres, etc.
- sticky notes to stick where you can see them
- a pinboard with pins, for photos, postcards, tickets, anything that inspires you
- a whiteboard with pens, for ideas that you can play with.

1

Starting out

Why have you picked this book? We all have a trigger point before
we decide to try writing a children's book. A book we read as
a child that made a deep impression on us. An image we can't
get out of our minds. A story we read in later years, to our own
children perhaps, that reminded us of that book that we loved.
A deep enjoyment of children's stories and the variety of worlds
and genres they offer, regardless of the age at which we discover
them. These are all great triggers. There is no need to question
them.

What we do need to question, however, is why *we* want to have a
go. It's important to be clear about our motives. That way, we know
where we are going before we begin.

 Hugh MacLeod, *Ignore Everybody:
And 39 Other Keys to Creativity*

*'Everyone is born creative; everyone is given a box of crayons
in kindergarten. Then when you hit puberty they take the
crayons away and replace them with dry, uninspiring books
on algebra, history, etc. Being suddenly hit years later with
the "creative bug" is just a wee voice telling you, "I'd like my
crayons back, please."'*

Why, oh why?

So, to come back to the question posed: why have you picked up this book? Let's dig into your psyche and see what we can find.

'I HAVE A GREAT IDEA'

This is an excellent starting point. I applaud you for already putting your imagination to work. It's exciting, isn't it, that feeling when you have a little kernel of gold in your mind that you feel sure will turn into something wonderful?

I'm afraid that having the idea is the easy part. Building that idea into something takes work. As Honoré de Balzac wrote, 'It is as easy to dream up a book as it is hard to write one.' You're prepared for that, right? You've picked up a 60,000-word book to help you get started on something that may end up 500 words long. That suggests the right kind of focus.

Ninety-nine times out of a hundred, an idea will wither on the vine, not because it's a bad idea but because the writer doesn't know how to nurture it. When the first flush of excitement passes, you can't see where it goes next. You struggle to visualize the span of your book. You can't make your characters sound the way you want, or look the way you imagined. Your story stretches to only one page and you don't know how to fatten it up. This is as true for experienced writers as it is for those just starting out. I would hazard a guess that every published author in the field of children's books has a drawer full of unfinished stories and half-sketched ideas that simply didn't go anywhere. You are in good company.

But this book isn't here to tell you to put your great idea away and go and do something more sensible instead. If you have an idea but don't know how to build on it, don't worry. Armed with the appropriate tools, it's entirely possible to turn your idea into something more three-dimensional. Maybe your first attempt won't work, but you will learn something by trying to make it happen. And you will apply what you have learned to the next great idea that you have. And then, a few years down the line, you may find yourself revisiting your original idea and crafting it into something better. I can't promise it will ever be published, but if you set your mind to it, there's no reason why it can't be finished.

Write down the idea that brought you to pick up this book. If you don't have an idea yet, think of something and jot that down as a starting point. Now consider the following:

- Do you want to illustrate it yourself?
- What age do you think will enjoy it?
- Is there anything in the bookshops that compares to your idea?

'MY IDEA HASN'T BEEN DONE BEFORE'

This feels different from 'I have a great idea'. It implies that you've studied the market very hard and have found a space on the bookshelves that you intend to fill or die in the attempt. Your story is called *Ernie the Line-dancing Earthworm*. Scissor kicks, invertebrates: this baby has it all! You haven't thought about the writing or illustrating part yet, but you feel confident that these are secondary to the originality of your concept.

You're on dangerous ground. There are only a finite number of plots, and they've all been done. Anything that remains generally remains unwritten for a good reason.

Georges Polti states that there are 36 plots in his book *Thirty-six Dramatic Situations* (1916). Christopher Booker's *The Seven Basic Plots* (2004) claims, unsurprisingly, that there are only seven. Other theorists have declared that there are just two stories: going on a journey, and a stranger coming to town. Which you could argue is the same plot really, just seen from the opposite direction. Anne Fine, prize-winning author and the UK's Children's Laureate 2001–3, has said that 'plots are overrated', and she may have a point.

Great children's books can be about nothing at all, and yet everything at the same time. The story that will succeed is not the madly original idea; it's the brilliantly well-constructed one.

Francesca Simon's Horrid Henry series, illustrated by Tony Ross, provides a great example of books where nothing much happens. We have two brothers, one horrid and one perfect, passing through their very normal lives at school, at home, in the garden and in their home town. On the face of things, the idea is quite boring. There are no line-dancing earthworms, no earth-destroying aliens, no wish-fulfilling fairies. And yet the series has sold over 14 million copies, with a TV series and a film to boot. Its success doesn't lie with the originality of its concept but with its rock-solid structure: strong, sympathetic characters overcoming problems within a clear narrative arc. Structure is something that we will be working on later in this book.

I'm not saying don't write about Ernie. I'm just gently pointing out that you need legs to line-dance. Unless perhaps Ernie's problem is that he *has* no legs? If so, that's a brilliant problem for a line-dancer. Maybe you can file this one under 'I have a great idea', after all. We'll come back to that.

'MY STORY HAS THE POTENTIAL FOR A SERIES AND MERCHANDISING'

A series is good. Publishers like to think long-term, and if they see you as someone with more than one book in them, that is a positive. However, limit your series ambitions to three or four titles. Publishers won't be thinking *that* long-term. And you still need to start with the basics: a good story, well told, with characters that children can identify with.

But merchandising – *whoa*. Why would anyone turn an unknown story into a range of lunchboxes? We have Gruffalo pencils because *The Gruffalo* has sold in excess of 10 million copies in 15 years. Rein in your ambitions. It's great to dream, but never approach a project with merchandising in mind.

Personally, I think Ernie would work well as a pencil. They share certain characteristics. But we are still some way from turning him into stationery.

Joan Aiken

'Anyone who writes for children should, ideally, be a dedicated semi-lunatic.'

'MY CHILDREN ENJOY MY STORIES'

There's nothing lovelier than the faces of your own children as you tell them stories. It is completely understandable as a motive for diving deeper into the world of published books.

I'm sorry to burst your bubble, but *of course* your children enjoy your stories. They are your children. They love the attention you are giving them when you draw pictures or read just for them. Perhaps they already know the characters, and the voices, and the actions, because they are based on something familiar: the neighbour across the road with the huge beard that you are all convinced is Father Christmas in disguise, or the fat family cat's secret exercise-bike regime. Your stories might have started in off-the-cuff desperation when your child is convinced there is a monster behind the curtains at three o'clock in the morning and the only way you can get them back into bed is to make the one-legged soft toy you once bought in an airport talk to the monster and order it back to Monsterland. With this kind of PR, how can you fail?

EXCEPT... there are millions of children out there who know nothing about Wonky the Wallaby. Who have monsters of their own that bear no resemblance to the one you've created. To them, your monster is thin and unremarkable and the teddy character is dull. Keep that humbling thought in mind as you read the rest of this book. But don't worry. Wonky may yet live.

Award-winning author-illustrator Emily Gravett used to read picture books to her daughter, and analyse them, and wonder whether she could produce something better. She enrolled on an art course to explore this idea. She got nowhere to begin with because, she says, she tried to follow the rules too closely. The moment she gave her own style a chance to develop, she produced *Wolves*, a book that went on to win the coveted Kate Greenaway Medal for children's illustration in 2005.

Incidentally, my own children couldn't care less about a single word I've written. Thank goodness I didn't listen to *them*.

'I WANT TO BE THE NEXT J. K. ROWLING'

J. K. Rowling's fame, riches and 1,500-million-odd book sales worldwide are a extremely rare by-product of great storytelling and good timing. Don't try to imitate her. Instead, be proud of your own voice and style and develop that. It's a shame to go into this field imitating what has gone before. Publishers are looking for innovation, not repetition. See Emily Gravett, above.

There are hundreds of brilliant, published, prize-winning children's authors out there who still have day jobs because they can't make a living from their books. They keep writing anyway, because they *want* to. They *have* to. They *breathe* their words and characters and stories. Forget about money and success. Find out what you like writing about, and write about it. If that's writing about wizards, go for it. Just be cautious about telling publishers that your book is the next *Harry Potter and the Philosopher's [Sorcerer's] Stone*. Like sprouts before mince pies, the story must always come first.

> ## Key idea
>
>
> An idea doesn't turn itself into a book without concerted effort. But if you are prepared to put in the time, you can produce piece of finished work. What happens next is up to you.

'I WANT TO PRACTISE FOR WHEN I CREATE ADULT STORIES'

Why plant apple pips when you want to grow oranges? Writing for children isn't a short cut to writing for grown-ups. It has a whole soil, climate and culture of its own and it needs your full attention. Maurice Sendak, whose *Where the Wild Things Are* is one of the most revered picture books of all time, may have said, 'I don't write for children,' but he's Maurice Sendak, and we, sadly, are not. There are plenty of brilliant books on how to get started writing books for adults that might suit you better than this one. Having said that, don't abandon us right away. Children can cope with most of the same themes that adults can. You may find that your idea is workable for children, after all.

Madeleine L'Engle

'You have to write the book that wants to be written. And if the book will be too difficult for grown-ups, then you write it for children.'

'I DON'T HAVE TIME TO WRITE ANYTHING LONGER'

It's true that children's books are generally shorter than adult ones. I once wrote a book containing just 17 words. But short or not – and there *are* children's books out there at 500 pages or longer (Philip Pullman's *The Amber Spyglass* weighs in at 518) – they still have to bear the full weight of readers' expectations: rich characterization, tensions, a well-built story arc, believable emotions. They take longer to create than you might imagine. And if your idea is good, you'll probably find yourself spending a long time on it regardless. So bang goes that plan.

'I HAVE SOMETHING TO TEACH CHILDREN'

The first book specifically aimed at children is probably *Das Kunst und Lehrbüchlein* by Jost Amman, published in Germany in 1580. The title page describes it as: 'A book of art and instruction for young people wherein may be discovered all manner of merry and agreeable drawings.' Although it uses encouraging words like 'merry' and 'agreeable', it was designed as a learning tool. Until relatively recently children's books were all written to improve young minds, with any hint of entertainment a by-product of that most important purpose. But time has moved on.

As adults, we're in the enviable position of knowing more than our children do. It can be satisfying to show the kids what life can be like if they do it right; how there is more to life than gadgets; how much better things were in the olden days. But preaching must be avoided. Children – and publishers – can spot it a mile off.

Snapshot

Think back to when you were a child. What did grown-ups lecture you about? Did it make any difference to the way you behaved? Write down your memories of those times.

If you feel particularly passionate about something and want to encourage readers to think hard about what you're telling them, you must be sneaky. Tell your story in such a way that the readers reach their own conclusions – or think they do. Your motive must lurk in the depths like the pike in the castle moat, not dance on the surface of the water shouting, 'Look at me!' *Where's the Elephant?* by the French illustrator Barroux is an almost wordless picture book about deforestation, conveyed *Where's Wally?* style where the children hunt for the different animals in a forest habitat that dwindles with every page. The children are so engrossed in spotting the animals that the environmental message sneaks in without them even realizing. Let your message reveal itself through your story and your characters, never through your narrative voice. It's like Aesop's tale of 'The North Wind and the Sun', and their bet about who could remove the traveller's cloak. The Wind blew so hard that the traveller clutched his cloak more tightly around himself. The Sun coaxed so gently that the traveller chose to remove his own cloak. The Sun won.

Always be the Sun.

If you want to write for yourself and nobody else, least of all children or publishers, you are of course welcome to ignore all of the above and write whatever the heck you want. But I'm working on the assumption that you want to see your name in print one day. Who doesn't?

Snapshot

Why do you want to write and/or illustrate for children?

Write down your reasons. Put them where you can see them as you work through this book.

Get reading

Ursula K. Le Guin

'There have been great societies that did not use the wheel, but there have been no societies that did not tell stories.'

Reading is the flipside of the writing coin. Without readers, writing is so much shouting into the void. Stories are meant to be told; that is their function. There is evidence of visual and oral storytelling throughout thousands of years of human history. The relationship between the storyteller and the audience is entirely symbiotic, with each side depending on the other for its existence. In other words, there have never been stories without audiences, and there have never been audiences without stories.

Darren Shan

'A book is a dance. Without the reader, the writer is just a lunatic twirling round by themselves.'

As stories made their way on to paper, they found a new kind of audience, known henceforth as 'readers'. This transition worried Socrates, who believed that writing things down weakened the power of the mind and the memory and spelled disaster for society. Similar concerns are being raised today as books make their slow transition from print to electronic format. What effect will it have on our youth to have so much information available at the press of a button? *Plus ça change*. Throughout the turbulence, the constant has always been the story. And the story, as children's author Darren Shan so neatly points out above, is nothing without its audience.

You want to write an illustrated children's book. So I must ask you a crucial question before we go any further. What was the last children's book that you read?

William Faulkner

'Read, read, read. Read everything – trash, classics, good and bad, and see how they do it. Just like a carpenter who works as an apprentice and studies the master. Read! You'll absorb it. Then write. If it's good, you'll find out. If it's not, throw it out of the window.'

If you want to write for today's children, it's essential to know what today's children are reading. You can't base your research on stories that you read and loved when you were a child. Biggles won't cut it. Enid Blyton won't either. You need to be reading books published in the last five to ten years. If possible, you need to be aware of what's about to be published, too, and what the powers that be think is the Next Big Thing: not so you can copy that Thing but so that you can get a sense of the domain you are trying to enter. If you use social media, follow authors, illustrators, publishers, book bloggers and librarians on Twitter and Facebook. Writing and illustrating books is a lonely existence, and these platforms offer us a social life. We talk about books we love and books we don't; events and prize-winners, schools and shortlists; pieces that we're struggling with, moments of celebration when work is finished. All of it is useful information if you are thinking about joining in.

Key idea

There is no writing without reading. To write well for children, you must keep up with current children's books by reading regularly.

Fiction categories

If you're new to the world of children's books, bookshops can be confusing places. What is shelved where? Which books are for four-year-old boys, or seven-year-old girls, or ten-year-old tomboys? Here's an outline of the main illustrated fiction categories that you will need to be familiar with. I have left out teen/young adult (YA) fiction as it is so rarely illustrated.

PICTURE BOOKS

- Age 3–7
- 1,000 words maximum; often 32 pages (layout is vital component)
- Large format
- Colour illustrations
- Aimed at parents to read aloud to children
- Examples:
  - *Goodnight Moon* by Margaret Wise Brown and Clement Hurd
  - *The Great Dog Bottom Swap* by Peter Bently and Mei Matsuoka.

YOUNG FICTION

(including reading schemes, reading series, series fiction and chapter books)

- Age 5–8
- 1,000–15,000 words
- Smaller format
- Colour or black-and-white (b/w) illustrations throughout (approximately 40 maximum)
- Aimed at new readers, in school or for pleasure
- Examples:
  - *Oxford Reading Tree: Biff and Chip* by Roderick Hunt and Alex Brychta (reading scheme)
  - Orchard Crunchies by various (reading series)
  - *Beast Quest* by Adam Blade (series fiction)
  - *Claude in the City* by Alex T. Smith (chapter book)

MIDDLE-GRADE FICTION (US TERM BUT FAMILIAR IN UK)

- Age 8–12
- 20,000–40,000-plus words
- Black-and-white illustrations, often chapter heads only
- Aimed at fluent readers
- Examples:
  - *The Secrets of Vesuvius* by Caroline Lawrence
  - *The Brilliant World of Tom Gates* by Liz Pichon
  - *One Dog and His Boy* by Eva Ibbotson

We will explore each category in more detail as we make our way through the book.

Snapshot

Find out the answers to the following.

- Name as many Children's Laureates as you can.
- Who won the Kate Greenaway Medal this year?
- Who won the Carnegie Medal this year?
- Who won Best Story in the most recent Blue Peter Book Awards?
- Who won the most recent Red House Children's Book Award – the only book award voted for entirely by children?

Find as many of these authors and illustrators as you can in your local library or bookshop, and read their work.

Workshop

Write a short review of one of the books you read in the Snapshot exercise above. Address the following:

- What was it about?
- Who was the main character?
- What was the theme/subject/genre?
- Did you enjoy it?
- Describe the style of illustration
- Describe the style of language
- Which of the categories listed above do you think it fitted into?

Next step

Now that you are more familiar with your motives for writing a children's book, the general categories into which illustrated children's books fall, and the books that are already out there, it's time to look at understanding your readers and how they see the world.

2

Be like your readers

What kind of child were you? Can you remember?

Our memories of childhood become distorted as we grow older. If you were to ask someone who knew you as a child to describe you as you were then, you may be surprised at what they say. Their descriptions of you may not match your own memories of yourself at all. You may wonder if the two of you are talking about the same person. You might remember yourself as a quiet and thoughtful individual, while the other person recalls you as someone who never stopped talking. Perhaps you think you always stood still while your hair was braided before school, when the reality was that half the morning you were being chased around the house with a hairbrush.

This distortion can spell trouble for children's writers and illustrators. Remembering how you truly were, not how you think you were, can make a difference in your storytelling. Getting it wrong can sound as false as the memories themselves.

❝❞ Jim Henson, creator of *The Muppets*

'The most sophisticated people I know – inside they are all children.'

What were you like as a child?

There are plenty of people who claim never to have cheeked a teacher or done anything silly when they were children. It's a common cry among parents across the land as they get their children ready for school in the mornings: 'I never had to be told five times to put on my shoes! I always brushed my teeth without being asked!' I can't help but wonder: did you really? You sound very dull. I wouldn't have wanted to read about you.

I recently asked my parents to choose three words to describe me as a seven-year-old. I chose the age of seven because it feels like the heartland of illustrated fiction: an age when you can enjoy picture books, reading schemes, reading series, your first chapter books and sometimes even a touch of middle-grade fiction. They came up with brainy, creative and lively. They are similar to the words I would perhaps use to describe my own children: generic and generous. But true?

When I think of myself at that age, I think in terms of isolated incidents at school: things that perhaps my parents weren't aware of. In other words, memories that are completely and specifically my own. The first memory involves leaving a game because it wasn't being played to my liking, thereby ruining it for my friends. The second is sticking my tongue out at a dinner lady I didn't like. The third is being caught looking up rude words in a dictionary at the back of the classroom. My three words are thus: bossy, defiant, curious.

The brainy, lively and creative child versus the bossy, defiant, curious one? I know which would be more fun to read about.

Key idea

Don't sentimentalize children or childhood. Don't be afraid to get down and dirty with the bad side.

Write

What were you like aged seven?

- Ask someone who knew you then to summarize you in three words.
- Now think of three things that happened to you when you were that age. Write down the incidents exactly as you remember them. Don't edit out the bad bits. Be completely honest.
- Select three words to summarize yourself, based on these incidents.
- Compare conclusions. Do you sound like two different people?

You can turn this exercise around and aim it at someone older than yourself as well, although this obviously requires imagination rather than memories. If asked for three words on how I imagine my mother to have been as a child – for example, I would probably say clever, stoical, well behaved.

At boarding school in the 1940s, my mother tells me she was always hungry. On one occasion, she smuggled a pie into school, balanced two wooden rulers on some upended tooth mugs, put a candle beneath the pie and attempted to heat it up. She almost burned the school down. That, my friends, is material.

Think young

To write well for children, it is important to be childish.

'Childish' has two meanings: 'Of, like or appropriate to a child' and 'Silly or immature' (*Concise Oxford English Dictionary*, 11th edition (2009)). Being childish in the first instance means that you understand what children find funny, what they consider sad, what they think is beneath them, what fills them with awe. Childishness encompasses everything in a child's experience: fear, delight, horror. It's not just about jokes. Childishness means that you aren't looking down on a child's curly little head, marvelling at how adorable they are while telling them how silly it is to cry just because there are no strawberry-flavoured Starbursts left in the packet. You are feeling what that child is feeling, most likely because you remember feeling that way yourself. If you can harness this childishness in your writing, use it to the hilt. It gives stories an honesty that can't be faked.

'Childish' in the second instance should be approached with care. There is nothing wrong with being silly and immature for a young audience, but you must be *aware* of this childishness. And that, of course, isn't childish at all.

> ## Key idea
>
> Being childish isn't the same thing as being funny. You don't have to write or draw humorously to have a childish outlook. Childishness covers every emotion experienced by children, from delight to despair.

Yvonne Coppard draws a useful parallel with an excited puppy off the leash (*Writing Children's Fiction* (2013) by Yvonne Coppard and Linda Newbery). The puppy is great at exploring, testing, experimenting, finding things you never expected it to find. But no one wants an overexcited little dog trailing mud over cream sofas and widdling in the porch. You need to keep the puppy under control, on a nice long lead. It then has the illusion of freedom, the chance to range away from the safe path – but that freedom is dictated by you. With one twitch, you can bring it back to heel.

Children might be anarchic creatures, but total anarchy in books bothers them. If they want silliness, they want it within safe parameters; sustenance, solidity, great characters and decent jokes that don't wear thin. Like adult readers, they enjoy stories by writers who know when and how to twist the mood without sounding shallow. Endless gurning punctuated with exclamation marks doesn't cut it. Children are quite capable of that type of silliness by themselves, wheeling around the playground as they pretend to be elephants or aliens. They expect more from you. You're the grown-up. Don't let them down.

Andy Stanton's Mr Gum books, illustrated by David Tazzyman, are a great example of comic childishness. They ramble. They are full of made-up words. They use impossible metaphors. They play around with all the conventions. The pictures are weird and spiky. But, despite the madness, you never get that sinking feeling that you're wasting your time and the stories are going nowhere. Childishness is there in abundance, but it is never uncontrolled. That's why it works.

Andy Stanton on www.mrgum.com

'I like Roald Dahl of course... Fantastic Mr Fox, The Twits, Jibberly and the Gribloff, *which is one that he wrote especially for me. I'm the only person to have ever read it, you can't get it in the shops. It's the best one actually.* Jibberly and the Gribloff *is fantastic. It's a thousand pages long and also some of the characters when you're reading actually come to life and give you presents but you can't read it because I've got the only copy.'*

The inner child

Time and again I read how authors and illustrators access this childishness when they create books for young readers. It is something that Yvonne Coppard describes as 'the abandonment to the moment'. Children are all about now. As former Children's Laureate and award-winning author Anne Fine puts it in her article 'Writing Books to Read Aloud' for *The Children's Writers' & Artists' Yearbook 2010*, 'A child of six isn't "disappointed that the weather is unpleasant". It's all far more immediate. He feels the tears pricking because his socks are wet and his woolly hat is itching and his coat's too tight under his armpits.' This immediacy is something that we lose as we grow older and realize that life isn't just about now, but about *then* and *next*; about how actions affect both present and future, and the importance of good decision-making.

Barry Cunningham

'We must always remember [children's] hunger for hope and a bright tomorrow, the closeness and importance of relationships – how easily a world can be upset by parents, or loss of an animal or friend – and the way in which action really does speak to children, for fantasy and adventure is part of the process of literally growing an imagination.'

An adult knows, perhaps from experience (I'm saying nothing), what happens if they act on that urge to eat an entire tub of ice cream, where a child does not. Children dive in with reckless abandon and guzzle the lot. They are bewildered when their small stomachs rebel. They are miserable to find themselves being sick in the middle of the night. They blame you, the parents, for the tragedy of their situation. But I didn't *know* it would be bad for me, Mummy. *You* knew. *You* should have stopped me. And you tell them that you did warn them, and they didn't listen, and next time perhaps they will think a little harder.

This inability to think beyond action to consequence is a common theme in children's books. There are countless stories out there about characters acting on the spur of the moment and regretting it. The characters might be old men, or hamsters, or princesses. It doesn't matter. What matters is the reckless act that gets them into trouble in the first place. Children recall with a shudder the twisting of their stomachs after that ice-cream tub, and nod, and feel wise, and want the character to come safely through the torment, just as they did.

The example that comes to mind is Ursula K. Le Guin's *The Wizard of Earthsea* (1968). Ged, the arrogant young magician's apprentice, dabbles in magic too powerful for his fledgling skills and unleashes a shadow creature from the world of the dead. The rest of the book is Ged's painful journey to confront the creature he released. Aged 12, I remember finding the scene where Ged summons the creature almost unbearable, because I knew it would spell trouble. But if Ged hadn't made that poor decision, there would have been no story.

You may think that spirits of the dead and too much raspberry ripple inhabit entirely different places in children's minds. They do not. Understanding this is a vital building block to making your characters and stories appealing to young readers.

'Childlike' is something else again. The dictionary defines it as 'having the good qualities, such as innocence, associated with a child'. Beware of being childlike. It's a creepy quality in an adult. By all means write stories about innocence and goodness, but keep the full weight of your adult sensibilities behind them or they will never work.

Snapshot

Think of a poor decision that you made when you were young. Write it down. How did it make you feel? What did you learn from it? Did you ever do it again?

Building imagination

Another key element of childishness – and a lynchpin for creating successful children's books – is the ability to use your imagination as you did when you were a child. Children have imagination in abundance; adults too often lose it.

Robert R. McCammon, US horror writer

'We all start out knowing magic. We are born with whirlwinds, forest fires, and comets inside us. We are born able to sing to birds and read the clouds and see our destiny in grains of sand. But then we get the magic educated right out of our souls. We get it churched out, spanked out, washed out, and combed out. We get put on the straight and narrow path and told to be responsible. Told to act our age. Told to grow up, for God's sake. And you know why we were told that? Because the people doing the telling were afraid of our wildness and youth, and because the magic we knew made them ashamed and sad of what they'd allowed to wither in themselves.'

I was driving to my parents' village a couple of years ago when I passed a field full of grazing horses. One of the horses was white. As I drove by, a gleam of light in the corner of my eye turned into a horn on the white horse's head. I turned my head in astonishment, but the light had disappeared and the horse was, once again, a horse.

The childish part of me knew I'd seen a unicorn. The grown-up part knew that I hadn't. The feelings have remained side by side in my head ever since, acknowledging each other without trying to argue the point. And that's fine. I write children's books. I'm allowed to see unicorns in my normal grown-up life. You are, too.

To some adults, imagination is a real and living thing that informs their lives and choices. To others, it feels frustratingly out of reach. Don't be downhearted. It isn't an irreversible process. Imagination is like a muscle. If you don't use it, it grows flabby. With a little exercise, we can have yours up to speed in no time.

Imagination is, as the football pundits say, a game of two halves: the sensory imagination and the inventive imagination. The sensory imagination is rooted in reality, where the inventive imagination spins away into strange worlds.

Our ability to visualize varies from brain to brain: a fact proved by a psychometrician named Francis Galton in the mid-nineteenth century. Galton's detailed surveys found that some people could picture objects in their minds, while others couldn't. The ones who could visualize had always assumed everyone could. The ones who couldn't had assumed likewise. Galton's statistics proved that there was, in fact, a wide spectrum of ability, from the about 5 per cent able to visualize in perfect detail (named 'hyperphantasia' in recent research conducted by Professor Adam Zeman at the University of Exeter Medical School) to the 3 per cent completely unable to form mental images (named 'aphantasia' in the same research). There are doubtless similar variables in our ability to recall sounds, tastes and textures. Wherever you are on the spectrum, your sensory imagination will still work at some level – and there is no reason why that level should adversely affect your ability to write children's books if you exercise what you have in a way that suits you.

Focus point

Imagination needs regular exercise to keep it supple and strong. Make sure you exercise yours.

Before you wail at me, 'I have no imagination, I never did and I never will!' let's be clear. *No one* has zero imagination. Everything in life requires aspects of imagination in one form or another.

Let's prove it.

You need to buy semi-skimmed milk. A single pint maybe, just to tide you over until the weekend shop. However you approach it, whether visually or via other means, your mind should be (at least in the UK) conjuring up a bottle with a green lid. Your sensory imagination exists, right there, synapses firing, producing a bottle of milk in the centre of your brain when plainly there isn't a bottle of milk there at all. All that's missing are the details: the condensation running down the sides of its opaque pimpled plastic skin, for example, or that chilled feeling that comes from wrapping your hand around it straight from the chiller cabinet, or the sharp ridge just beneath the handle that prevents your fingertips from getting entirely comfortable. If you let your mind linger on that pint for long enough, those details will emerge. You are now exercising your sensory imagination.

Snapshot

You have a doctor's appointment this afternoon. You decide to use a familiar car park because it's just a short walk to the surgery from there. Pause and allow your mind to expand through the details. Don't worry if some senses work more strongly than others in this exercise: this is about 'seeing' things in whichever way feels most real to you.

SIGHT Is the car park large? Irregularly shaped? Is there a pothole that you always mean to avoid but invariably don't? Are the meters new, are the cars old? Is it busy with families, or pensioners, or workmen? Is it multi-storey, underground or open to the elements? Are the spaces small? If you want to extend this, picture it by day and night, in the rain and the sun and the frost.

SOUND Does the road surface change as you swing in, making a different sound beneath your wheels? What does it sound like when you hit that pothole? If it is an enclosed space, do you get an echo when you slam the car door?

SMELL/TASTE What is the air like when you park that little bit too close to the bottle bank? Can you smell the fumes from the other cars? Is there an unmentionable stink in the stairwells?

TOUCH Do you burn yourself on the car door when it's hot? Do your fingers adhere to the metal in the winter? Are the buttons on the parking meter greasy? Do you feel the jolt through your whole body when you hit that pothole?

Snapshot

Here is an exercise to help you improve visualization:

- Draw three shapes – a blue square, a yellow triangle and a red circle – on a piece of paper.
- Study them, then shut your eyes and bring them to mind. Open your eyes to refresh your memory whenever you need to. Practise until they are clear.
- When you are ready, you can colour them differently, render them in three dimensions, or move on to something more complex, like a flower.
- Repeat daily.

Follow-up

Walk around the place where you live. Then try to repeat the exercise while opening and closing your eyes at intervals, allowing your mind to 'see' what's there when your eyelids are down. Please don't fall down the stairs on my account.

You're feeling cheated. Shouldn't we be focusing on the invention aspect of imagination and conjuring up fairies and kittens? What child wants to read about a pint of milk?

Remember what I was telling you about childishness, and rooting yourself at the level of your readers. Don't assume from your lofty adult position that because children are children, they automatically want fairies and kittens. Just like adults, children want good stories, well structured and imaginatively told, with characters and situations that they can relate to. They *can* be about fairies and kittens, but they don't have to be. Take Neil Gaiman's book *Fortunately, the Milk…*, illustrated by Chris Riddell and published by Egmont, which was the Sunday Times Children's Book of the Year 2013. It's about a dad who pops to the shops for a pint.

 Key idea

There is a huge difference between writing what adults think children want and what children want for themselves – and, in children's books, that translates into the chasm between success and failure.

The inventive imagination is more elusive than the sensory one, although it is founded on experience in much the same way.

Fortunately, the Milk… is, of course, about considerably more than just that pint of milk. On his way to the shop, the dad is abducted by aliens before falling through a wormhole into the eighteenth century to land in a pirate ship, travelling a thousand years further back into the past in a hot-air balloon in the company of a time-travelling stegosaurus, meeting scary 'wumpires' and avoiding the end of the universe by the tip of his Tetra-Pak. No wonder it takes him so long to get back home.

The book is a great example of the extraordinary rooted in the ordinary: one of the great traditions of children's books. A writer or illustrator will often take a child's ordinary experience, easily recreated by judicious use of the sensory imagination – home, school, friends, family – and then riff on it through the inventive imagination, asking questions, wandering down peculiar, unexpected alleyways that real life simply doesn't allow for. The inventive imagination is where the fun really starts.

Focus point

The inventive imagination is rooted in the sensory imagination. If your sensory imagination is strong, you can use your observations and recollections to invent alternatives. That's why it's vital to exercise your sensory imagination every day.

The speed of change

Children change quickly. This is something you may have noticed in your own children, or among children you know. 'How you've grown!' is a sentence I always promised myself never to say to a child, but it is impossible to swallow the surprise when a short span of 18 months turns a familiar little boy into a gangling pipe cleaner.

Their reading tastes change, too. A book that appeals to a three-year-old will be too young within a year to 18 months. A six-year-old might read something aimed at ten-year-olds but, because of the limits of their age and experience, are likely to miss several layers of meaning, while a ten-year-old will probably ignore something aimed at a six-year-old because they will feel such stories to be beneath them. Children's understanding of the basic tools of storytelling – vocabulary, grammar, humour – is constantly expanding. In the space of a few short years children can make the jump from simple linear stories of home life to complex multi-stranded plots set in strange worlds. In no other field of fiction do readers change so much, so fast. You have a window of two to three years before your intended readership moves on. It can be dizzying. We'll look more closely at the different age levels further on in this book, and help you get to grips with the approach that's right for you and your idea.

Who is buying?

As well as developing a nose for fitting the right story to the right age level, you also have to factor in who will be *buying* your story.

Unlike the adult market, books for children aged 3–12 are not often purchased by their intended audience, but by the 'gatekeepers': parents, grandparents, teachers, librarians, aunties and uncles, and the full gamut of grown-ups invested in your readers' lives. You have to find the balance between 'fun' and 'suitable' that these gatekeepers will be watching out for.

Workshop

For the 'three words' Write exercise earlier in this chapter you came up with three incidents from your childhood. Choose one to work on now.

- Use your sensory imagination to expand your account, just as you have practised. Zoom in on the details: sights, sounds, smell and taste and touch. Add these details to your writing.
- Now use your inventive imagination to develop one aspect of your account which didn't happen. See how seamlessly you can blend it into the rest.

Next step

Now that you have practised what it is to be childish and started flexing your imagination, we'll move on to the question most people ask published authors: where do you get your ideas from? In the next chapter we'll take a look at how to use the world around you, how to extend your sensory and inventive imagination, and how to crystallize your ideas.

3

Finding ideas

Imagine a town, high in the Alps, say, where you can just pick up an idea. How easy it would be! You could choose from a million, all of which would be bestsellers. You might even start a bidding war among competing publishers, all falling over themselves to publish you as you smile for the flashing cameras in your hotly anticipated press conference.

But beneath the smiles, wouldn't you feel a tiny bit guilty? You picked up your idea from someone else. Your bestselling idea isn't yours. Wouldn't it be better to develop something that you thought up all by yourself? From experience, developing your own ideas is preferable to developing other people's. You are more invested in making them work.

Where ideas come from

But where *do* you get your ideas from, if not from the Forka Pass?

This is the most common question on the creative writing circuit. I get a terrible urge to shout 'House!' whenever it crops up, before hunting around for my bingo card so I can cross the question off. It has become invested with enormous significance. It is seen as marking the boundary between success and failure. The room falls silent as everyone strains to hear the author's answer. Tell me your secret! What's the password? Where's the treasure map?

KLAXON. There's no secret, no password, and no map. Authors get their ideas from the same place as you do: life. And then they struggle to flesh them out as much as you do. Very occasionally, a fully formed idea will come strolling into an author's head – a certain train-conceived wizard leaps to mind – but it's rare. On the whole, we're all in the same boat.

Personally, I don't think people ask, 'Where do you get your ideas from?' because they're interested in the author's ideas. They ask because they're interested in their *own* ideas: how to find them and use them and turn them into bestsellers. And rightly so. If you don't take an interest in your own ideas, who will? So next time you're tempted to ask an author that question, turn it round and ask instead: 'Where can *I* get *my* ideas from?' And that's something that I hope to help you answer in this chapter.

Authors get other questions, too, by the way. After I had shown a group of children a photograph of a far-flung galaxy that resembled a penguin guarding an egg, I was asked, 'Is that penguin dead?'

 Key idea

> Anyone can have an idea. The secret of success lies with the development of that idea, not the idea itself.

The spark

You need to think of ideas as sparks, set at the foot of a bonfire. The bonfire is big and will take a while to burn. It's likely to be damp, with non-flammable and/or toxic material lying hidden at its heart because you popped to the bakery for a doughnut just when that shifty skip lorry was driving past. It will probably also contain hedgehogs, which must be removed with gloves.

Putting the bonfire together the right way is just as important as the spark that will set it alight. But, of course, the spark has to happen or the bonfire will remain a dark and uninteresting heap of sticks. (And there's still a hedgehog in there. I can hear it moving around.)

 David Almond

> *'Allow yourself to experiment, to play, to be surprised by what appears on the page.'*

To make a spark, you need a flint. To make an idea, you need to engage the sensory and inventive imaginations discussed in Chapter 2. Like a spark, an idea can appear and disappear within the same moment. It's worth keeping a notebook and pen with you, or a tablet, or some means of jotting down ideas as they flare into life. Authors are always prepared to catch and pin down that fleeting thought. And now, so are you. That piece of advice alone is worth the price of this book.

Don't worry if you struggle to develop these thoughts beyond a jotted line or two. It's all good practice. Most ideas don't go anywhere, but you might find with practice that you get one or two that are workable. You just need one spark, and you can begin.

Professor Piper from *Fangirl* by Rainbow Rowell

'Start with something real. With one day from your life. Something that confused or intrigued you, something you want to explore. Start there and see what happens. You can keep it true, or you can turn it into something else – you can add magic – but give yourself a starting point.'

A firework of ideas

In keeping with this autumnal theme, let's move from bonfires to fireworks.

When a firework bursts into life, it sends out stars that explode into smaller stars, and then, if you're lucky, stars that are smaller still. Just as the most multifaceted firework starts with a single bang, so an idea for a story can start with a single word. I cheated you all in Chapter 2 by talking about pints of milk, so let's talk about something more traditional this time. How about monsters?

You may feel that we are starting at a more advanced place than we were with a pint of milk. You can conjure a pint based on real-life experience, firing up that sensory imagination we were practising in the previous chapter. Can you conjure a monster in the same way? Aren't we leapfrogging the sensory part of the imagination with monsters, and plunging right into the inventive bit?

We create monsters from our own experiences, too. All we are doing is extending those experiences, and perhaps blending them together. We are more likely to give a monster a lion's head, a vulture's neck and a snake's body than some shape and texture we have never seen or experienced for ourselves. Think of monsters as second gear, where milk is first.

So. To build my word firework, I will first write down 'monster'. I'll then think of three words associated with monsters. I'll pick one of these three words, and think of three more associated with that. I'll repeat the process a couple more times until I end up with a piece of paper covered in words; a night sky full of sparks.

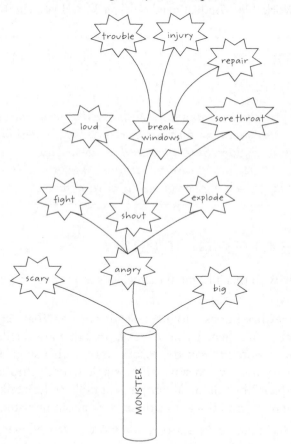

From just one word, 'monster', I'll now have 12 associated words or phrases to play with. How about 'Monster, big, sore throat'? or 'Monster, punch, injury'? The inventive imagination can start to develop a huge monster who has been shouting so much that he has lost his voice, and an injured monster in an accident and emergency department scaring the nurses. Two ideas, just like that.

If you think visually, you could try to build your firework with images instead.

Write

- Put the name of an animal (zebra, wombat, etc.) at the centre of your word firework.
- Think of three words associated with that animal.
- Think of three words associated with one of those words.
- Repeat twice more.
- Write a sentence using your animal and two selected words from your firework.
- Put it somewhere safe. It could be the start of your first story.

Asking questions

To develop ideas for children's books, it's important to be curious in the way that children are curious. Why do wasps have stripes? What does Queen Elizabeth wear in bed? Don't be afraid to ask yourself questions, and don't be afraid to answer yourself in as strange or charming a way as possible. The great joy in writing fiction is that *you don't have to tell the truth*. No one will challenge you if your explanations are odd. In may cases, the odder the better. My father always cites a question he once heard a boy ask another boy a very long time ago.

'What's a geek?'

'He's the guy in the poultry factory who sucks the farts out of chickens.'

Rudyard Kipling

'I have six honest serving men
They taught me all I knew
I call them What and Where and When
And How and Why and Who.'

Rudyard Kipling famously used these six questions to trigger thoughts and ideas in his writing. I would suggest expanding 'What' to another writer's favourite, 'What if?', as in 'What if horses were purple?' Asking negative questions is another trick: 'Why aren't...?' and 'Who isn't...?', for example.

You can apply these questions to anything, and then let your imagination take over. If the thought of engaging your imagination here makes you nervous, look back at the exercises in Chapter 2. We all visualize and invent every day of our lives. All we are doing here is transferring those everyday thoughts to paper or screen.

Workshop

Look out of your window. Can you answer any of the following questions about what you can see?

- Why is/isn't that happening?
- How did that get there?
- When did that happen?
- What if that wasn't there?
- Award yourself extra marks if you succeed in making yourself laugh.
- Add sketches if you would like to.

Daydreaming

 Thomas McGuane, *The Longest Silence*

'The slackest line catches the biggest fish.'

Our resting brains store all kinds of extraordinary things. Images, feelings, words and phrases lurk in our little grey folds, waiting for a chance to emerge. They can be triggered by music, or smells, or can simply float into view unannounced, like a dream I had in which one person inexplicably said to another: 'And then I woke up in the coffin, covered in gingery eyelashes.' Our subconscious is working constantly when we are least aware of it. It's one of our greatest assets when it comes to generating ideas.

I was a dreamy child, and I am a dreamy adult. I frequently baffle my husband by failing to answer a question directed at me two or three times because I'm in my own world. My eldest son has the same tendency to drift away to somewhere else – a place that only he sees and only he inhabits.

Daydreaming is an essential part of an author's toolkit, and should be actively encouraged. Be absent. Stare into space. There is value in giving your brain a chance to churn in peace and solitude. Go for walks. Take time. Lie on the grass and gaze at the sky. Study beetles crawling over leaves. Swimming works for me. I start off with a head full of to-do lists, but after 20 lengths or so I'm somewhere entirely different. When the brain is at its most relaxed, ideas will often settle into your consciousness like a fat trout on a hook.

Orson Scott Card

'Everyone walks past a thousand stories every day. The good writers are the ones who see five or six of them. Most people don't see any.'

The Internet, too, is perfectly adapted for authors stuck inside on rainy days, staring at a sentence that refuses to take shape and wanting to shriek with frustration. Writing is a solitary occupation and you need release. This is what I tell myself when I emerge blinking from half an hour on boredpanda.com. A cat riding around the kitchen on a robot vacuum cleaner? An elephant that paints portraits? It's all grist to the brain mill.

If you hook something, get it down in that notebook I told you to carry with you at all times (you're reaching for it now, right?). Then you can build it from there at your leisure, in ways I have already shown you: make a firework with words from your initial concept, or ask questions that will make you see the idea from as many angles as possible.

A word of warning, though: don't spend too long in la-la land. Look at what happened to Rip Van Winkle.

Doodling

Chris Riddell

'Stories can grow out of the visual. It can be an engine for literacy.'

Doodling is another version of daydreaming. Just as writers keep a notebook for ideas, artists keep a sketchbook for thoughts and ideas that occur to them. Chris Riddell, the UK's Children's Laureate from 2015 to 2017, started a daily logbook of sketches when he began in his role. A sketchbook keeps the brain and fingers limber, poised and ready to pounce when the great idea arrives. The illustrator and cartoonist Ronald Searle sketched constantly when he was studying at the Cambridge School of Art, until, in his words, 'the habit of looking and drawing became as natural as breathing'. No skill need be involved. A mindless scribble can trigger ideas as much as a carefully considered sketch. It's all a manifestation of what's going on inside your brain. Capture it in any way you can.

Liz Pichon's hugely successful Tom Gates series is about a character who is defined by his doodling. His sketches embellish every other word on the page, lending visual interest to the stories and breaking up the text. There are a number of successful young fiction series like Tom Gates that are approaching stories in a much more visual way than in the past, with pictures threaded throughout the text. *The Diary of a Wimpy Kid* by Jeff Kinney and the Big Nate series by Lincoln Peirce are other examples.

Snapshot

Doodle something on a piece of paper. To make this exercise more interesting, close your eyes as you do it. Does the doodle resemble anything? Does it set off any thoughts in your mind? (My attempt produced 'Old man in cloud of smoke'.)

Work with what you know

What do you do in your working life? Are you a teacher, a police officer, a shop assistant, an athlete? If you are retired, what *did* you do? Is there anything you're passionate about: trains, stars, your local football club, horses? You may not consider yourself an expert in either your professional life or your personal interests, but the undeniable truth is that you know more about your own world than I do. Your life is material. If you're a teacher or a dinner lady or a caretaker, think about setting a book in a school. If you're a fisherman, give us a sea or river story. Mine your experiences. By using what you already know, you're ahead of the game.

If you can see no way of using what you do in your everyday life, it's worth reaching out to people who are in regular contact with children and picking their brains. Teachers and librarians, especially school librarians, are fantastic resources. They could probably give you any number of child-related incidents every day for a year, and still have stories to tell.

Kurt Vonnegut

'We have to be continually jumping off cliffs and developing our wings on the way down.'

Inspiration

A common misconception is that writers waft around all day until inspiration decides to settle on them like some kind of benevolent moth. This is not true. We waft for perhaps 10 per cent of our time – see daydreaming, above. The rest of our working hours are graft. They have to be, or we'd never get anything done.

Waiting for inspiration to strike can be boring. And becoming aware of your passivity can cause panic. 'I'm not doing anything. I'm not creating anything. There are no sparks, no bonfires, no fireworks. I promised myself on New Year's Eve that I'd have a workable idea by Easter, and I still have nothing more than a few scribbled word fireworks and a handful of weird questions… How can I make this happen faster?'

If you are entering the writing life with a view to making a living, you can't afford to dawdle. Sometimes you need to give inspiration a shove in the small of the back. Strike the right balance between daydreaming and actively tickling the trout on to your hook, and your chances of coming up with workable ideas will improve.

 Jack London

> 'You can't wait for inspiration. You have to go after it with a club.'

Inspiration is everywhere. Curious headlines in newspapers and magazines: 'Squirrel found resembling Abraham Lincoln', for example. Eavesdrop on buses, in supermarket queues, everywhere. I once overheard two men at a music festival earnestly discussing dragons. Liz Pichon lifted an anecdote about a misbehaving garden hose by football manager Harry Redknapp straight from the radio and gave it to Tom Gates's dad in *Yes, No, Maybe*. Listen, observe, write it down or sketch it out. Keep it somewhere safe. You never know when it might come in useful.

Randomize

A great way to kick-start inspiration is to use a random sentence: a verbal doodle, if you like. Type 'random sentence generator' into your search engine and you will be directed to websites that might set something off in your mind. Alternatively, put your faith in your own subconscious and pluck out the first sentence you think of. Use whatever comes out, however odd. Answer all the questions that it poses.

When I did this, I once got: 'It started with the octopus on the landing.' Immediately, there were a dozen questions needing answers. What started? Where did the octopus come from? Why was it on the landing rather than, say, on the kitchen table? Was it poisonous? How big was its tank? *Was* there a tank?

By using Rudyard Kipling's technique of questioning, you can turn a random sentence into a story. You can make inspiration come to you.

Focus point

Sometimes you have to invite inspiration into your head. It's not enough to wait for it to knock.

Words or pictures: which come first?

Martin Salisbury, *Illustrating Children's Books*

'When putting together a picture book, the final form of the words is often the very last piece of the jigsaw.'

Geraldine McCaughrean

'[A picture book is an opportunity] to lay fourteen and a half visual opportunities in the lap of an artist.'

Illustrator, journalist and lecturer Professor Martin Salisbury states several times in his excellent book *Illustrating Children's Books* that story ideas invariably start as visual. Geraldine McCaughrean, a multi-award-winning author, clearly thinks that the story begins with the words. Who is right?

Alex T. Smith, author and illustrator of the Claude books, describes the whole as a joke, with the words as the set-up and the pictures as the punch lines. Both elements have to work *together*. The most successful illustrated books are those where words and pictures harmonize as a single unit. As with reading and writing, the relationship between words and pictures should be one of *symbiosis*.

'Symbiosis' is a word I often come across when reading about the relationship between fungi and woodland. It means a mutual relationship, with each partner relying on the other to maximize its own potential. Illustrated books should be symbiotic in the same way. The relationship changes when you move from picture books into the more text-heavy environment of young fiction and beyond, but it still needs to be there. Each element should extend the other in some way. The whole, to steal a phrase, should be greater than the sum of its parts.

The easiest way to achieve this harmony when creating a piece of illustrated fiction is always to bear the words in mind as you sketch out your ideas, and think about the visual aspect as you jot down your thoughts. It's difficult, but not impossible – a bit like rubbing your tummy and patting your head at the same time.

Allan Frewin Jones and Lesley Pollinger, *Write a Children's Book and Get It Published*

'If a heroine is wearing her favourite red scarf, the only comment needed in the text is that it is a favourite, and not that it is red.'

Chris Raschka

'I always try and treat the book itself as the artwork. I don't want you to stop while you're reading one of my books and say, "Oh! What a gorgeous illustration!" I want you to stop at the end of the book and say "This is a good book."'

Write the following words slowly. Pause after each line and visualize what you have written.

- A red ball.
- A bouncing red ball.
- A huge, bouncing red ball.

Consider how adding a word changes the way you visualize what you are writing. Add more words. Take the exercise as far as you can.

This exercise works from a visual perspective, too. Draw a simple picture of a flower, then build the image, visualizing words to describe each stage.

Visual creative or word nerd?

Perfect symbiosis is the ideal, but not everyone naturally strikes the middle ground when imagining stories. I tend to think of text first, while I have an artist friend who thinks in pictures. Neither of us is right or wrong. We both just have to make adjustments.

Judith Kerr

'Unlike all my other stories, I had thought of [The Tiger Who Came to Tea] *only in words, not in pictures, and I wondered whether it should wear clothes? Or a hat? Happily I decided against it.'*

Chris van Allsburg

'At first I see pictures of a story in my mind. Then creating the story comes from asking questions of myself. I guess you might call it the "what if – what then" approach to writing and illustration.'

So how do *you* approach ideas? Do thoughts and conversations set you off, or do your light-bulb moments happen when you see pictures? I blogged this question a few years ago: are you a visual creative or a wordy one? Take the quiz to find out.

Snapshot: quiz

1 You see a picture of a little girl crying her eyes out on a fabulous beach. Do you:
   a Report the photographer to Social Services?
   b Locate the spot on Google maps with a view to holidaying there?
   c Attempt to paint it but struggle to find the right shade of cerulean?
   d Write it down?

2 Someone pins a picture of your latest book cover on the highly visual social media website, Pinterest. Do you:
   a Celebrate?
   b Try to repin but forward it to the Venezuelan Embassy by mistake?
   c Attempt to crayon a version of the cover on a tablecloth?
   d Write it down?

3 You find a mystifying, swirly image online that you can't work out. Do you:
   a Ask for clarification from the source?
   b Rush for the acrylics and design a sarong based on the same colour principles?
   c Decide it looks like baby sick?
   d Write it down?

I did try Pinterest once. My favourite picture was a map of Portugal composed entirely of the words 'This is not Spain'.

Writer's block

Willie Nelson

'My mind was blank. All I could do was look around and say, "Hello walls". That was probably a stupid way to start a song, but what the hell? It was better than nothing.'

(In 1961 'Hello Walls' went to number 1 on the country charts and sold 2 million copies.)

You've tried word fireworks, Rudyard, randomized sentences. You've eyeballed beetles, drawn endlessly variable flowers. You've even been fishing, with wet feet to prove it. Nothing is coming out. You don't know where to go next. You feel like hurling this book across the room with considerable force and taking up crochet instead. You have a classic case of writer's block.

Writer's block is not terminal. You can break through the wall. It's just a question of understanding where your brain has come off the rails, and working out a way of lifting it back on to the track.

Louis L'Amour

'Start writing, no matter what. The water does not flow until the faucet is turned on.'

Gestalt theory holds that the brain follows a cycle of experience. In their paper 'Gestalt: a philosophy for change', Trevor Bentley and Susan Congram liken this cycle to an ocean wave. The wave starts from deep in the sea – a point known as 'the fertile void' – before moving upwards through the stages of awareness, energy and action. It crests, surges forward, and dies a natural death on the shore before the cycle begins again.

We are all trying to surf that wave. We need the 'fertile void' to kick-start the process. We need to reach the crest of the wave before we can ride it to its natural, fully satisfying conclusion. But we often can't generate enough energy to reach the top of the wave. The rest of the cycle is then denied to us. We have to watch the wave curl and crash away from us. Our aim is thwarted, our desire frustrated. We are left with unfinished business.

Naturally enough, we wonder if there is an easier way. A brainstorming session, a pick-up-the-ball-and-run approach. Brainstorming can fall foul of this 'wave-hopping' approach if pursued too quickly. Without the rise and fall of the proper cycle of experience, brainstormed ideas often don't get a chance to take root. By skipping from the crest of one wave to another, never investing the energy to surf the wave from start to finish, you are moving through a void more futile than fertile. This often translates as writer's block.

The good news is that, in the immutable laws of the ocean, another wave will be along in a minute. Paddle harder than last time. Go deep. Write anything. Draw anything.

Write

Try it now. Glue yourself to your chair and write ten lines of nonsense. You can do that because you have fingers and paper, a pencil and a keyboard. Do what you can to reach the top of the wave. Then you can start enjoying the ride.

J. K. Rowling

'I've no idea where ideas come from and I hope I never find out; it would spoil the excitement for me if it turned out I just have a funny little wrinkle on the surface of my brain which makes me think about invisible train platforms.'

Next step

*In the next chapter we will look at the tricky issue of genre – the
kind of book you are writing. Some writers baulk at the idea
of tailoring their work to a specific genre, but publishers (and
bookshops, real or virtual) certainly like books that can be fitted
into one. And, in fact, genre can offer you, especially as a new
writer, a structure to work with – and that can be liberating and
even inspiring.*

4

Genre

Subject and theme are different things. **Subject** is very specific: you're writing about otters, or basketball, or skyscrapers. **Theme** is waftier: an overarching concept, an impression of something greater than the story, such as friendship, jealousy, family.

The easiest way to remember the difference between the two is to think in terms of *before* and *after*. Subject matter should be in place *before* you set pencil to paper or finger to keyboard, while theme should emerge *after* a story has been created. It's important to get this distinction right. If you think too hard about your theme before you start, it can overpower the story, and before you know it your manuscript has been relegated to the 'preachy and boring' pile. Whereas if you don't think hard enough about your subject before you start, you *have* no story.

There are literally *millions* of subjects out there for you to write about, and thousands of themes hanging around the fringes of your subconscious. There are so many that it can seem frightening as you gaze into the abyss and wonder where to start. It may be easier to think in terms of **genre** instead and this is what we will focus on in this chapter.

Genre: what kind of story?

Meg Cabot

'Write the kind of story you would like to read. People will give you all sorts of advice about writing, but if you're not writing something you like, no one else will like it either.'

Genre is the framework into which you can place your theme and subject matter. Some people stick their noses in the air and claim that genre is limiting. From a purely practical point of view – and practical advice is what you're after, I assume, since you are reading this book – I disagree. When you are learning a craft, it is useful to give yourself limits. It can free you from that paralysing cloud of wondering, 'What can I write about?' Find a genre that you like, and you are more likely to move forward and find subjects and themes within that genre that will suit your style and interests. When you've written a few books, and maybe even had them published, then you can play around with genre. Mash your ideas up. Go wild. But for now – stick with me.

Here are some examples of genre.

HISTORICAL

This can be tricky with picture books because young children are only just getting to grips with life in the present. If history interests you, you might be better approaching a story as a myth or legend (see below). Young fiction historical books are better, but still difficult. Your idea has to focus on something that modern children can relate to. Character is a vital way in. *Hetty Feather*, written by Jacqueline Wilson and illustrated by Nick Sharratt, is set in 1876, but is very much driven by the *character* of Hetty Feather and not the *time* in which her story is set.

War fits into the historical genre. It isn't generally a suitable topic for a picture-book text, but can work if handled carefully. Illustrator Michael Foreman and author Michael Morpurgo have both explored war in books such as *The War Game* (Michael Foreman alone) and *The Best Christmas Present in the World* (Michael Morpurgo and Michael Foreman together), focusing on the child-friendly Christmas truce football game in the trenches in 1914. They have also used animals to good effect, tackling the Spanish Civil War in *Toro! Toro!* through a boy whose pet calf is destined for the bullring, and the First World War in *War Horse* and *Farm Boy* through Joey the horse.

However, if you're interested in writing a war story, I would suggest avoiding the First and Second World Wars unless you have a particularly unusual angle. These twentieth-century conflicts are almost at saturation point in the market. Equally, don't pick a war so local or obscure that it offers no interest to the wider world. And always remember that you aren't telling the story of the war itself, but the story of the people involved.

Snapshot

Can you think of an anecdote or story about war relating to an animal or a child?

Write it down. It might be the kernel of an idea for you to develop.

TIME TRAVEL / TIME SLIP

'Time travel' is a slightly longer, more involved process than 'time slip', but they are essentially the same thing: people moving from the present to the past, or the present to the future. Rather like the historical genre, time travel/slip books can be problematic at a picture-book level because of the complexity of the idea. Any genre that requires elaborate explanation won't work in 1,000 words, the maximum amount of text in most picture books. However, you can have fun at a young illustrated fiction level, as long as you don't let yourself get bogged down in the detail at the expense of the story. *Dinosaur Cove* by Rex Stone is an example of the time-slip genre for this age.

SCI-FI/FANTASY

Aliens are great for young fiction but often find success in picture books, too. Nick Butterworth's *Q Pootle 5* has recently been turned into a television series, while *Aliens Love Underpants* by Claire

Freedman and Ben Cort has spawned several spin-offs. In young fiction, I have a series called Space Penguins packed with aliens (and penguins); Bruce Coville's *My Teacher is an Alien* still works brilliantly 25 years after it was first published. My only word of warning: keep it low-tech. Kids generally don't care how the rocket works, as long as it delivers the characters into the alien-packed action.

Fantasy can be problematic at the picture-book level if the reader needs too much information to make sense of the story, with so few words in which to deliver both background and plot. As with historical and time-travel books, anything that requires 'world building' or complicated explanations about kingdoms and borders and supernatural powers should probably be avoided for this age. The supernatural is difficult in picture books anyway, for international market reasons. Magic and fairies are covered in what I would call the traditional tales genre, which we look at next.

TRADITIONAL TALES

Given that it has been at the heart of children's storytelling for hundreds of years, it's difficult to find a traditional tale that hasn't been done to death. That said, if you can find an original slant on an old story, you may be in with a chance. Eugene Trivizas and Helen Oxenbury's *Three Little Wolves and the Big Bad Pig* is a great example of this.

This genre can be broken down further into:

- **Fairy tales:** 'Cinderella', 'Sleeping Beauty' – we know them all. These almost always involve kings and queens, princes and princesses, magic and happily-ever-after endings.
- **Folk tales:** These have make-believe elements but are rooted in real life, for example *The Enormous Turnip*.
- **Myths:** These are set in the distant past, and are often about gods and impossible feats, for example Michael Morpurgo and Michael Foreman's *Beowulf*.
- **Legends:** These feature the embellishment of real or fictitious lives, for example *The Legend of Frog* by Guy Bass.
- **Fables:** These are short stories or poems with moral endings. Aesop is generally given the credit for inventing this genre.

Religious

The religious genre is difficult in international markets, and often rejected straight away for this reason. It is also almost always a case of finding a specialist publisher. If you really want to write in this area, I would suggest approaching religious stories in much the same way as I have suggested approaching fairy/folk tales: try to find a fresh angle. *Jesus' Christmas Party* by Nicholas Allan is a terrific example with the Nativity told by the disgruntled innkeeper ('Round the *back*!'), while Michael Morpurgo and Quentin Blake's *On Angel Wings* tells the story from the point of view of a shepherd boy.

Adventure/mystery

Classic territory for children's books at this age, adventure essentially means a fast-moving plot with lots of excitement and a smattering of red herrings, where characters get themselves into and out of scrapes before resolving the mystery in a satisfying manner. These days, adventure is more often found blended with other genres, as in Caroline Lawrence's historical Roman Mysteries series or Cressida Cowell's fantasy/historical series How to Train Your Dragon. Interestingly, it's easier to think of pure adventure-for-the-sake-of-adventure books from 30 years ago than it is to think of modern titles, but a series like Helen Moss's Adventure Island seems to have picked up where Enid Blyton left off. Adventure is an area that lends itself particularly well to series, a subject that we'll be looking at later on in this book.

Focus point

Another warning here. Don't rehash five gung-ho kids solving mysteries without asking yourself: do I have anything new to add? Publishers don't want to see a shadow of Enid Blyton. They want to see and hear *you*. Robin Stevens's Wells and Wong series, about two girl detectives in a 1950s boarding school, may sound Blyton-esque in outline, but modern grit and self-awareness turn it into something different, which is why it works.

Bear in mind that picture book adventures are tougher to write than young fiction, as picture-book storylines need to be clear and linear with very little room for red herrings or subplots.

Horror/ghost

This is a tough one for picture books. Ghosts aren't popular in the international market for lots of different cultural reasons. Plus parents may not thank you for scaring their children before bedtime. If you want to have a go at a scary story, make sure that it relates directly to a small child's experience – fear of the dark, for example – and then make sure that you approach it with love, humour and a very happy ending.

Horror used to be very successful in young fiction with R. L. Stine's Goosebumps series. But it was always horror with a silly or humorous twist. Perhaps its time will come again.

Poetry/rhyming story

Firstly, you should note the difference between poetry and rhyming text. True poetry is rich with imagery, rhythm and words. Rhyming text diddly-diddly-diddles along. Neither is an easy sell, but poetry is the tougher of the two.

First of all, there is the issue of translation: those all-important co-editions with other countries that make the difference between profit and loss on a full-colour publisher's balance sheet. That pesky international market is notoriously difficult to please, even when the translation is straightforward. When the words have strict rhythm, rhyme and imagery to deliver as well as everything else – yikes. Even that simple couplet embracing 'dog' and 'fog' doesn't look so hot in French – *chien* and *brouillard* – or German – *Hund* und *Nebel*. Not only does it no longer rhyme, it doesn't even share the one-or two-syllable rhythm so vital for making poetry scan. Translation of poetry texts takes longer and is subsequently more expensive.
In such a risk-averse industry, publishers may feel your rhymes just aren't worth the effort.

Now that I've well and truly put you off, don't let me put you off. Just go into your chosen genre with eyes wide open and be prepared for perhaps more rejection than most. It helps if you are a published poet already, or a poet with a good track record of performance. You may also have an edge if your work celebrates specific dialect or patois – although, ironically, this makes the translation question even tougher. Benjamin Zephaniah published his first children's poetry book, *Talking Turkeys*, a full 15 years after first making it into print with an adult collection. Valerie Bloom's *Fruits: A Caribbean Counting Poem* illustrated by David Axtell is a retelling of an existing poem, matched with vibrant pictures full of Caribbean flavour.

Case study: *A Squash and a Squeeze* by Julia Donaldson and Axel Sheffler

Category: Picture book

Genre: Rhyming story

What is it about?

An old lady in a small house asks a wise old man to help make her house bigger. He suggests taking her hen, goat, pig and cow into the house. When he tells her to get rid of the animals again, the house feels gigantic.

The relationship between the words and the pictures

The words came first, starting as a song for *Playschool*, a mainstay of children's television in the UK in the 1970s and 1980s. It was only when Julia was approached by a publisher ten years later that it became a book. Because it evolved this way, Julia hadn't written it with pictures in mind. The illustrations are very attractive, but I think they accompany the text rather than work with it.

Julia and Axel have worked on books together for 20 years, but they don't work collaboratively. Julia presents Axel with the complete story, and Axel draws it. Likewise, Axel has no idea what the story will be about until then, and he works around what he's given. In his original illustrations for *A Squash and a Squeeze*, Axel drew the old lady with lots of wrinkles and a pointed chin, but the editor asked him to make her rounder and cuddlier. Julia has occasionally made allowances for Axel's drawing preferences when she creates stories. She knew, for example, that he had grown sick of drawing trees after *The Gruffalo* and *Monkey Puzzle*, so she set *Room on the Broom* in the sky to give him some variety.

Voice

The story's origins as a song are very evident. There is a repeated chorus: 'Wise old man, won't you help me please? My house is a squash and a squeeze' and regular repetition of 'Take in your hen/goat/pig/horse,' said the wise old man, 'Take in my hen/goat/pig/horse? What a curious plan'. The words were designed to be sung, so have great internal rhythm.

Write

Read *A Squash and a Squeeze* yourself and write a short review, considering each of the points above from your own perspective. How successful is the relationship between text and image? How is the story enhanced by the use of rhyming text? Could it have been told just as well in another way?

Humour

Terry Pratchett

'You can't build a plot out of jokes. You need tragic relief.'

All children love jokes. Surely, this is a safe bet for your first children's book? This genre does offer lots of fun, but it is tricky. Humour is very specific to its country of origin and often fails to translate. Something you find hilarious might offend others, or leave them baffled. Humour should be avoided if it's coming at the cost of a well-thought-out story.

Children also find different things funny at different stages in their development, so it's difficult to pitch humour at the right level. A one-year-old finds a game of peekaboo the most hilarious thing in the world. At two, nonsense words and sounds seem to tickle children's funny bones: bish bash bosh! At this age, they also appreciate the fun of changing the natural order: put your shoe on your head and your toddler will roar because they know it ought to go on your foot. Three- and four-year-olds love bathroom humour, perhaps because they are in the process of mastering the big loo themselves. Five- and six-year-olds are beginning to read and are learning that things don't have to be as they seem. This is the age when children start 'getting' more complex jokes, enjoying wordplay and visual trickery.

Children enjoy humour at every stage of their development, but it's important to keep it at the right level or you will lose your audience. Always judge your tone and the balance of your story before you jump into the jokes.

Animals

The children's book market is dominated by animals. Mice, lions, bears, penguins – stories about these creatures are everywhere. Why?

Firstly, animals are cute. A book with a kitten on the cover sells a lot of copies. Secondly, animals translate better in the international market than humans – and we have already discussed how important the international market is for picture books. And thirdly – perhaps most importantly – stories about animals aren't stories about animals at all. They are stories about children.

There have been some phenomenally successful animal books for this age group in recent years, not least the Animal Ark series featuring books like *Kittens in the Kitchen* and *Bunny on a Barge*.

The original covers featured the main character, Mandy Hope, alongside the animals of the title. Uptake wasn't as good as the publisher had hoped, so they took Mandy off the covers and made the animals bigger. Sales instantly rocketed. In short: done right, animals sell.

Snapshot

Do you have a favourite animal? Does it have any child-like attributes that you could use in a story?

Character-driven

This is worth a whole chapter by itself. In fact, that's exactly what I'm going to do. I shall simply mention a few classic character-driven picture and young fiction books here for you to bear in mind – the series Charlie and Lola, Paddington, Hugless Douglas, Big Nate – and work on this subject further in Chapter 5.

Matt Haig

'There is only one genre in fiction, the genre is called book.'

Other factors

While genre will provide the main scaffolding for your story, there are several other factors to consider as you write. Areas such as diversity and how to approach difficult issues such as illness, bereavement and so on need to be handled with sensitivity and tact and, sometimes, courage. Don't be afraid to broach these things but take some precautions, too, especially when you're high up on that scaffold.

DIVERSITY

 Leila Berg

'Every child needs to be able to look at a book or hear a story and feel, 'That's me!' This is what every middle-class child has done practically since babyhood.'

I don't want to isolate diversity as theme, subject matter or genre because an awareness of it should be threaded through everything you write. But it's important to talk about it. Diversity in children's books still falls woefully short of where it needs to be to reflect a true picture of modern society.

Recent statistics show that one-fifth of children in the UK have black or other ethnic heritage. A 2015 report from the National Literacy Trust found that black girls are among the UK's most prodigious consumers of literature, with 16 per cent saying they had read ten or more books in the previous month. These are figures that are in no way matched to the number of books starring black or ethnic minority characters. I specifically use the word 'starring', not 'featuring'; the black sidekick or Asian best friend has become a lazy writer's habit that needs further thought.

There are gender imbalances as well as ethnic ones. A 2011 report into children's fiction between 1900 and 2000 found that male animals featured as central characters in 23 per cent of books per year, with their female equivalents languishing at 7.5 per cent. There is a long-held belief that boys will not read books about girls, while girls will happily read about boys – a belief which needs to be challenged in the twenty-first century. And too many of the girl characters that have successfully made it out there are described as 'feisty' – a word that makes me shudder. 'Feisty' is never used to describe boys. 'Feisty' suggests that your girl is only a successful female character because she plays hardball, but she'll never be as good as a boy because... duh. Positive girls, yes. Feisty girls, no.

Disability also needs more champions. Quentin Blake's *The Five of Us* features a group of children described as having 'special abilities' who have to rescue their bus driver on a school trip. 'We can't have a quota and we can't have a token,' he said in a BBC video interview in 2014. 'But one day I hope it just comes naturally, it's not something I would have to think about.'

Many writers, particularly first-time writers, feel nervous about approaching ethnically diverse or disabled characters. There is a fear that, if they aren't, for example, Asian or disabled themselves, they can't write about Asian or disabled people. They'll get into trouble. It's a minefield out there, they worry. What if they get the details wrong? I don't think this is a valid reason not to try. Any author who has created a vampire or a talking teddy bear will tell you that you don't have to have personal experience of a character's life and background to make that character believable. The key to success lies with empowering your characters so that they aren't defined by their disability, sex or skin colour. In my series Scarlet Silver with illustrator Sarah McConnell, Scarlet's little brother Cedric wears splints on his legs that are full of cunning Swiss-army-knife gadgets. More than once, his gadgets come to the rescue of more able-bodied characters.

Publishers are aware of the imbalance. They actively seek books that represent a more diverse society in the right sort of way. So be fearless. Do what you can to redress the balance. Like with anything in life, don't be crass. Don't bludgeon readers by shouting, 'Look at this character! She's BLACK! She's DISABLED!' Just be aware that diversity is important and there are children out there waiting for books where, for the first time in their lives, they can be the stars.

ISSUES

Much like diversity, issues can be threaded through any subject or genre, but must be done with a light touch. No one needs to be aware that they are reading a book about a tough subject like bereavement or divorce. Just as with any book, an 'issue' book has to invest its energies in the characters and plot and still deliver a satisfying reading experience: the 'issue' aspect doesn't lessen this responsibility. Susan Varley's Badger's Parting Gifts deals well with grief and loss because of its gentle language, delicate artwork, believable characters and uplifting ending. Judith Kerr does it beautifully with Goodbye Mog as well.

Never assume that children can't cope with difficult ideas. Children's books can and do cover pretty much every aspect of the human experience. Tone is the deal breaker at this level, not subject matter.

Having said that, picture book publishers are notorious for playing it safe. As in so many modern businesses, this all comes down to profit and loss.

Once upon a time, publishers simply published stories that they liked, with any foreign market editions seen as a bonus rather than a basic requirement. They published all kinds of things with absolute impunity, and often with titles we would now consider sexist, or racist, or plain inappropriate. This is no longer the case. In the modern publishing world, the international market – partners in what are known as 'co-editions', or versions of the same book published in multiple languages – is so vital for their profit margins, a picture book publisher will think twice before touching books whose subject matter may offend other cultures and markets: the supernatural, sex and romance, class, religion, horror, alcohol, drugs, gratuitous violence, junk food (yes, honestly). There are always exceptions that seem to brazen it out, but this is something to bear in mind when you are wondering what to write about.

For the same reasons, take care when writing anything with a local flavour, too: double-decker buses for example, dialect and traditional costume often fail to translate. Recognizable buildings and landscapes must be avoided. Localized animals don't go down well either.

Focus point

Try to think internationally *at all times* when you are creating a picture book. Going back to an earlier comment I made: why make getting published any harder than it already is?

Key idea

Picture books have strict boundaries. If you cross them, be prepared for a more difficult journey to publication.

A million stories

The sheer scale of what can and can't be written about is breath-taking. Don't let yourself be overwhelmed by it all. A story is just a story. It really can be about anything you like, particularly if you are just writing it for your own enjoyment. These areas are simply here for you to consider if you don't know where to start, with a few warnings along the way about potential pitfalls if you are serious about getting your work published one day. Your story won't stand or fall based on its subject matter, but on the strength of its characters and plotting.

Workshop

Consider the following ideas. Match them to the genres discussed in this chapter.

- A boy's pet pigeon is commandeered for pigeon post during the Second World War.
- Two girls discover a time-travelling bicycle.
- A boy's house is burgled and his grandfather's gold watch is stolen.
- A girl is given three wishes.
- Small green aliens kidnap a princess.

You may find that the ideas fit several different gonres.

How could you include diverse characters in these ideas?

How could any of these become 'issue' books?

Wait. Someone's saying something.

'My idea doesn't fit into a category. It's an all-ages, all-interests kind of thing…'

There are exceptions to the categories, of course, because where's the fun in always sitting neatly in boxes? If your idea is truly uncategorizable, however, then self-publishing is probably the best way to go, and the very best of luck to you.

But I would firmly advise a first-time writer aiming to catch the eye of a traditional publisher in much the same way I would advise a first-time swimmer: question your urge to take that lilo into the deep end before you are confident that, should it all go wrong, you can make it back to the side without drowning or being bombed by a screaming adolescent. Don't give yourself too much to do at this early stage.

Next step

In Chapters 5 and 6 we'll return to the different categories of children's books – picture books, young fiction, middle-grade fiction – that we touched on earlier, and see if we can make sense of them. When the divisions are clear in your head, you should be able to see more clearly where your idea will fit.

5

Picture books

As I said in my introduction, when most people think of children's books, the glossy, shiny, colourful, share-at-bedtime zone of the picture book is often what they have in mind. Perhaps this is because they are so enjoyable for both reader and listener. They create a shimmering bridge between generations, giving each side something to treasure. The child learns new and colourful things, while the reader returns to a time and place when life was simpler. There is real value in a book where you can pore over details and colours and characters together with a loved one and forget everything else for a little while. Picture books are pretty Zen, when you think about them like that. No wonder they are so popular among first-time writers.

Leaving aside the world of books for babies and toddlers – a realm best left to a publisher's in-house writers and editors – we will take a closer look at the heartland of picture books: stories for children aged 3–7.

66 99 Deborah Halverson, editor, Harcourt

'A great picture book will bring the generations together, every time.'

Brands and licensing

Before we explore the ins and outs of picture books, I'm briefly going to flag up the issue of brands and licensing.

The modern world is driven by marketing and product placement. Brands and logos dominate the high street; film franchises spawn endless repeats of themselves; films of books and books of films proliferate like ants on a picnic doughnut. Publishing isn't immune to this, as any sweep of a picture-book department in a bookshop will testify. Publishers' front lists are full of licensed products such as Peppa Pig, Thomas the Tank Engine and Minecraft. If it's on TV, online or in the cinema, the chances are that the 'property', as it's known, has been turned into a book. Not necessarily a good book – the text is often quite thin, the writing run-of-the-mill, the illustrations computer-generated – but a book nonetheless.

Branding and licensing works on a different plane from the rest of children's publishing. Publishers have entire, separate departments dedicated to this market, selling on every platform imaginable. It can be disheartening to visit your local bookshop and see nothing but Disney and *Fifi and the Flowertots*.

How are you supposed to compete?

Don't try. Just do your thing, and do it well. Perhaps one day your story will become an industry. But that day isn't yet, and thoughts of it shouldn't claim one iota of your focus.

Practicalities

Let's take a look at some of the physical aspects of picture books before indulging in the fun that goes with creating them. It's good to familiarize yourself with your tools before you begin.

HOW MANY COLOURS?

Full-colour printing – the whole rainbow of shades that you associate with picture books – was invented around the end of the nineteenth century. Prior to this, laborious, expensive hand-colouring was the only way. The printing process typically uses four coloured inks: the primary colours cyan (blue), magenta (red) and yellow, and the 'key' holding it all together: black. It involves four runs through a printing press, where these colours are laid on top of each other. The process is also known as CMYK, with the colours applied in that order. The 'key', black, is the last colour to be applied.

You can find two- and three-colour picture books, too. Ian Falconer's *Olivia* is printed in red and black, while young fiction books like the Claude series by Alex T. Smith, *Dixie O'Day* by mother-and-daughter team Shirley Hughes and Claire Vulliamy and *Squishy McFluff* by Pip Jones and Ella Okstad add blue or yellow to the mix.

Black is always used for the type. Only in very rare cases will you find picture book texts printed in red or blue. This is because, as the last colour to be applied, black is the cheapest to change. And publishers will change it as much as they possibly can, for as many different markets and in as many different languages as possible.

These 'co-editions' are crucial. Colour printing is considerably more expensive than black-and-white, so a full-colour book that can be printed for ten different markets will be a lot more attractive to a publisher than a book specific to one language or culture. It's rare for a publisher to take a picture book unless they can see some kind of international market for it. Incidentally, British English, Australian English and US English are, in the publishing world, considered different languages, and a black-plate change is required in exactly the same way as if the book were translated into Basque or Finnish. Strange but true.

HOW MANY PAGES?

Before you spend too much time on your hundred-page or seven-page picture book, you need to know that printing presses work in multiples of 8. Most standard picture books are 32 pages long. They are printed, folded, stitched or glued together in sections, and trimmed into the book shape you're thinking of. One press of the printing button equals 'cheap' – or, at least, as cheap as printing in full colour ever allows. Your 40- or 60-page book may feel the perfect length to you, but to a publisher it means an extra printing expense best avoided.

The layout of that 32-page book is very specific. There is always a lone page at the start and at the end, with the rest known as double-page spreads. There are usually 12 double-page spreads in a 32-page picture book, with pictures arranged to suit the way the pages fall. Anthony Browne, the UK's Children's Laureate from 2009 to 2011, always starts projects by drawing twenty-four rectangles and thinking of his books as film storyboards. Quentin Blake also creates storyboards on one sheet of A4 (known as *un chemin de fer* – a train – in French).

Take a look at the model opposite. Get to know it. Bear it in mind from the moment you have that great idea for a picture book that you want to see in print.

Case study: *Goodnight Harry* by Kim Lewis

Goodnight Harry is a story about a little elephant who can't get to sleep until his friends Lulu and Ted help him to relax. Let's divide up this story into a classic 32-page layout and study the outcome.

Page 1: The half-title page. Walker Books uses this as a kind of 'name plate' page for a child to write their name in the book, but it often features the name of the book.

Pages 2–3: A double-page illustration of the scene outside Harry's little wooden house. It sets the night-time scene, and introduces the owl that we hear partway through the book. It also sets the tone with the illustration style, which is soft and calm and quiet. There are no words because, technically, the story hasn't started yet. (Of course, it has started really, as any child enjoying the book will tell you.)

Page 4: The imprint page. This is the page at the start of a book covering publication information, text and illustration copyright details, dedications, perhaps a small picture, where the book has been printed (China, in this case), a list of numbers telling you having many times the book has been – or expects to be – reprinted and other important business details, all in uniformly tiny print. You don't have to worry about any of this, but you do need to leave a whole page free in anticipation.

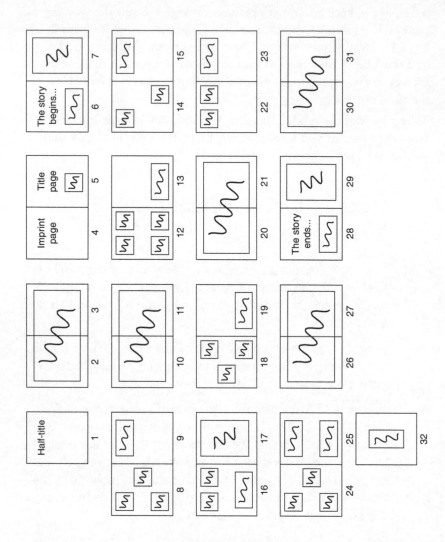

A classic 32-page layout for a children's picture book

Page 5: The title page. The book's name is featured, along with the author/illustrator and publisher. There is also a picture of the main character, Harry.

Page 6–29: Text joins the story, although it features only on 19 of these 24 pages. Pictures vary from double-page spreads for the most important sections to smaller vignettes, and from full pages to single-page images framed in white. The words never crowd out the pictures but are widely spaced on the white pages throughout, or placed in the pale-blue background of the five double-page spreads where there is no white space to be had. There are lots of ways to play around with layout in this central part of the book, but this shows a good range of approaches.

Pages 30–31: A repeat of the double-page illustration from pages 2–3, rounding off the story.

Page 32: A page advertising Walker Books.

What do you know? It's a perfect fit.

Snapshot

Find a recent 32-page picture book and analyse it as shown above. I would recommend looking at a book that has won a prize such as the Kate Greenaway Medal. Use the research that you did for the snapshot exercise in Chapter 2 to find a suitable title.

- On which page does the story start?
- How many double-page spreads are there?
- How many pages feature only text?
- How many just have pictures?
- How many combine the two?

Amy (age 5)

'I always remember pictures. I sometimes forget words.'

'There are picture books without text,' wrote Jean E. Karl in her 1995 book, *How to Write and Sell Children's Books*, 'but there are no picture books without pictures.' This is no longer strictly true. US comedian B. J. Novak wrote a picture book called *The Book with No Pictures* in 2014. As the title suggests, there isn't a single picture in it. Text, widely spaced in in different colours and font sizes, make up the visual element. The reader is instructed to read aloud every single word, no matter how silly. They have to say things like 'BLORK' and 'My head is made of blueberry pizza.' It doesn't tell a story, it just has lots of fun. Is it a picture book? 'Type is type, but it's also a picture,' said Dave McKean at the 2014 Seeing Stories conference. But I think Novak's book is the exception that proves the rule. Pictures are integral to picture books.

A picture book is often defined as a book where at least 50 per cent of the story is told via illustration. This ratio tends to drop as a reader grows older, with illustration veering away from the mainstream towards the more specialized area of comic books and graphic novels. But whether a book is 90 per cent or 10 per cent text to illustration, the pictures should always share the burden of the storytelling.

Lewis Carroll, *Alice in Wonderland*

'What is the use of a book,' thought Alice, 'without pictures or conversation?'

Far be it from me to discourage any enthusiastic artists out there who are champing at the bit to draw pictures to accompany a story they want to create. After all, I cannot draw at all. I did an onion at school once, which still hangs in pride of place in my mother's kitchen – but I suspect it's not there on artistic merit. I must draw your attention back to the warning I gave in the introduction to this book: ninety-nine times out of a hundred, even if your text squeaks past the gatekeepers and you achieve the Holy Grail of a publishing contract, those accompanying pictures you drew will be discarded.

Quentin Blake

'Guinea pigs are quite difficult to draw, I think, because they're so furry.'

The importance of well-drawn pictures for the children's market cannot be overstated. For 'well-drawn', read 'trained artists only need apply'. Children's books may be for children, but they are rigorously scrutinized and judged by adults. Anything less than art-school perfect will fail. You must trust me on this. Unless you have a degree in illustration *at the very least*, those pictures over which you pored so lovingly and for so long will simply not make the cut.

It isn't a question of being able or unable to draw. There are essential questions of design to answer as well. It's no longer a world of 'one page text, one page picture' as in Roger Hargreave's classic Mr Men series. These days, picture books mix it all up. If you want to illustrate a modern-day picture book, you must have the whole concept of the book in your mind's eye from the outset: every page, every angle. This is extremely difficult to achieve, even if you have spent three years training in illustration. You are expecting a great deal of yourself if you plan to do it from scratch.

Let's take characterization. Character is a crucial component in a children's book. There is a whole chapter on creating characters later (Chapter 7).

So. You have drawn an adorable mouse as your main character. One picture, one character. Right?

Wrong. Just as you can't make a written character come to life just by giving him a name, you can't create a character with just one picture. Your character has to move, progress, change, be a part of the whole from start to finish. Your single illustration of a mouse is only the tip of the iceberg. If he is the main character, you will need to draw him multiple times and from multiple angles – face on, sideways on, from behind, from above, large, small, running, still, half off the page, half on – in order to maintain interest. He'll be popping up a lot, and you don't want the same picture over and over again. Can you be certain that he will be identifiable from each and every angle? Will readers understand that the mouse on page 5 is the same mouse as the one on page 8, even though the first drawing shows him smiling and the second one doesn't? When is he worth a quarter-page, a full page, a double-page spread?

Do you see the difficulty? And this is just the beginning.

The truth is that a picture book is never illustrated until the whole book has been designed. The designer will create a **layout**: this is where various spaces are left for text and pictures on the pages. Sometimes those spaces will be big, sometimes small. Only when the layout has been agreed and the number of vignettes or full-page illustrations has been decided, will an artist will produce **roughs** (loose, sketchy illustrations) to suit requirements. The image s/he will produce will vary depending on how large the space is, how important to the story each picture is, and where and how each image will fit with the story's trajectory.

Focus point

A book is a bespoke suit, not a crumpled one-size-fits-all dishrag. No two books are the same.

When everyone is happy with the look and feel of the layouts, the roughs are added. Now the publisher can start to get a genuine feel for how the book will look when it is finished.

The layouts will then probably change. So will the text, in order to accommodate the urgent space which has appeared on page 8, or the sudden lack of room on page 16. This is likely to happen several times. The roughs will be tinkered with over and over again. Some will be discarded, some new ones will be added. Finally, the go-ahead is given – and the fully fleshed-out mouse strides into the pages he has been designed to fit.

The pitfalls for inexperienced illustrators are manifold. One common mistake is to place a large image, such as a face, across a double-page spread, where the seam of the page will swallow the nose and leave you with something very odd. It's essential to keep any important details of your pictures away from that central gutter – a crucial feature on a treasure map, an item mentioned in the text. Because of the way picture books are glued or stitched together, the central part of any double-page image will always vanish. Another is forgetting that all books are cut to a specific size and putting your images too close to the edges, where they will get lopped off. There are countless other rules and regulations which I cannot pretend to understand – and that's OK, because I'm a writer, not an illustrator.

HOW MANY WORDS?

Picture books are designed not to be read by their audience but to be read aloud by adults, often at bedtime or in those brief, snatched moments that small children give you. Unlike adult books, a successful picture book will also be read over and over again – sometimes two or three times in one sitting. In practical terms, a book longer than 1,000 words can take a while to read from start to finish. A book that is too long will often lose the attention of its young audience. If you have a story that you think will work as a picture book but is weighing in at 2,000 words or more, you have two options. Cut the text down to suit the picture-book format, or rework it for the young fiction market instead. Publishers won't do this for you. You need to match their requirements, not the other way round.

The ratio of pictures to words varies hugely within the age range of 3–7 that picture books cover. Very young children don't yet have the mental agility to leap straight from a word like 'revolting' or 'furious' or 'wonky' to the visual image the writer is trying to create. This is where the pictures do their work. A child reading a wordless book like Quentin Blake's *Clown* (on which more in a moment) will read the pictures first, bringing words such as 'funny' or 'sad' or 'running' to mind later. As a child gets older and starts to enjoy the texture and rhythm of new and exciting vocabulary, the text plays a greater part.

Key idea

Good picture-book text should say very little, while good picture-book illustrations should say a great deal.

As beginners dipping your toes into this world for the first time you should be thinking in terms of a sliding scale, depending on the age and interest of your audience. As with so much in life, this does of course come with a caveat: a book with few words but complex pictures will send a book further up that sliding scale than a first glance might suggest.

Year of publication	Book	Author/ (illustrator)	Words/ (pages)	Age
1998	*Clown*	Quentin Blake	None (32)	3+
2006	*Orange Pear Apple Bear*	Emily Gravett	5 (32)	3–5
1994	*Picture Book*	Ian Beck	32 (48)	3–5
1997	*Willy the Dreamer*	Anthony Browne	100 (32)	4+
2011	*I Want My Hat Back*	Jon Klassen	251 (40)	4+
2004	*How to Catch a Star*	Oliver Jeffers	377 (32)	4–7
1994	*Something Else*	Kathryn Cave (Chris Riddell)	529 (32)	4–7
1969	*The Elephant and the Bad Baby*	Elfrida Vipont (Raymond Briggs)	863 (32)	4–7

Key idea

The ratio of words and pictures generally works like a sliding scale according to the age and interest of your audience.

Clown by Quentin Blake was published in 1998. It tells the story of an unwanted toy clown tossed into a garbage bin along with his friends, who through optimism and determination finds a new family for himself and the others.

Taking into account a clown's talent for mime, Blake decided against using any words at all. This foxed the book buyers at the time, who weren't sure how to 'read' a book without any text. He talks about *Clown* in a 2009 video for teachers and parents on his website, www.quentinblake.com. The interview offers a fascinating insight into the way a picture book like this is created.

S. F. Said, Seeing Stories Conference 2014

'Forget the words and try and tell a story with a single image.'

Snapshot

Tell the following story in three quick sketches. It doesn't matter if you can't draw. This isn't about artistic skill, but about storytelling. Don't panic. You are the only person who will see these sketches.

- A child throws a ball for a small dog.
- The small dog runs after the ball.
- The small dog meets a big dog with the ball already in its mouth.

Tell yourself the story. What details might you add, if you wanted to embellish it? Remember: no words allowed.

(When I attempted this exercise for myself, my child was a stick person and my dogs looked like kangaroos. So no pressure.)

The next example on my list, Emily Gravett's *Orange Pear Apple Bear*, uses just five words – the four in the title and a final rhyming 'there' – but still tells a story through the bear as he balances, juggles and ultimately eats the fruit of the title. *Picture Book* is more of a vocabulary book than a storybook, but Ian Beck encourages the reader to build stories around what is happening in each image. Both of these offer a good example of illustrations playing a much greater part than words, and brings us back neatly to the work we did on sensory imagination feeding into inventive imagination (see Chapter 2).

Willy the Dreamer by Anthony Browne is proof that pictures can make a book much more complex than the relative paucity of words would suggest. Each image is surreal, imaginative and strange, and every page invites you to linger.

Next up is Jon Klassen's *I Want My Hat Back*. At first glance it doesn't look very exciting. The design is minimal, the colours sludgy, the vocabulary simple and the story subtle. And yet it gets funnier with each reading, building towards a great bear–rabbit stand-off that says so much but uses no text at all.

There is subtlety in Oliver Jeffers's book *How to Catch a Star*, too, but the visuals are more traditionally eye-catching. I cited Oliver Jeffers's background in my introduction: an author-illustrator who shot to fame and fortune via the slush pile. His first book, *How to Catch a Star*, is firmly in the centre ground, with an even balance of words and pictures.

Dr Seuss (Theodore Geisel)

'So the writer who breeds more words than he needs, is making a chore for the reader who reads.'

The last two books on my list of examples are Kathryn Cave and Chris Riddell's *Something Else* and Elfrida Vipont and Raymond Briggs's *The Elephant and the Bad Baby*. *Something Else* sets two strange little creatures against each other and invites them to see that they have more in common than they might have thought. *The Elephant and the Bad Baby* brings us an ever-expanding string of furious shopkeepers chasing the thieving Elephant and the Bad Baby 'rumpeta, rumpeta, rumpeta all down the road'. Words play a greater part than the pictures in these books.

When books get longer, they become more nuanced. At this level, it's rare to find books created by one person, because the weighting of the story is different. As with the examples, they are more often the work of two people: an author and a separate illustrator. With 500 words or more to work with, the text becomes more challenging, which is where a writer's specialized skills come to the fore. The illustrations usually follow the words and are designed to support and extend what's already there. The illustrator has a very different relationship with a book when it is created in this way.

What makes picture books successful?

What makes these books successful? Some of them weren't first books, that's true. Anything with Quentin Blake's name on it tends to sell; the same can be said for Julia Donaldson and many of the others. But even these stalwarts had to start somewhere. They were once standing where you are now, wondering the same thing: how do I create a story that will catch a publisher's eye?

CHARACTER

The creative process for Quentin Blake's *Clown* began with the character of the clown himself. After several drafts, Quentin Blake settled on a little figure with expressive, skinny limbs and painted eyes but none of a clown's traditional glumness. This is a crucial element in the development of the story, because the little character's optimism drives the plot. Without it, you know that the clown would never have wriggled out of the dustbin and set off for help in the first place.

Emily Gravett's bear is awash with watercolour cuteness. Ian Beck uses the same character of a little boy to tie a series of otherwise unconnected pictures together. Anthony Browne is well known for his trademark characters, Willie the chimp and Hugh the gorilla, both of whom feature in *Willy the Dreamer*. The contrast between Jon

Klassen's naive hat-owning bear and sneaky hat-stealing rabbit drive us strongly through *I Want My Hat Back*. Oliver Jeffers connects us with his characters through his affecting visuals. *Something Else* couldn't work without the two odd little souls at the heart of the story (not to mention the third, even weirder one who shows up on the last page); the ungrateful Bad Baby is so terribly rude. More than words, pictures, or combinations of both, stories ride on the strength of their characters. Character will be explored further later in this book.

WHAT ISN'T SAID (OR SHOWN)

The success of *I Want My Hat Back* lies as much with what isn't said or shown as with what is. The more you read it, the more you see. You have the pleasure of spotting the hat thief well in advance, seeing through his babbled denials before the bear does, and grasping why the bear sits alone at the end of the book, wearing his hat and a furtive expression while denying all knowledge of hat-wearing rabbits. Its hidden layers give the brain a richer workout than if you were to lay everything out on the table from the start.

Clown clearly doesn't 'say' anything, giving you endless variations on how you tell the story. Emily Gravett's bear subtly changes shape and colour to match the fruit in the title. Both Anthony Browne and Ian Beck allow the mind to wander through a variety of stories, using the pictures as springboards. And even though I have read *How to Catch a Star* a hundred times, I still wonder if the star is real, or if it's simply a reflection in the sea or an ordinary starfish.

If you want to write a book that will be reread 50 times before a child tires of it, bear the notion of hidden layers in mind. It makes the repetitive reading experience more of a pleasure. It might even make the difference between someone buying your book and not. I'm sure I'm not alone in browsing picture books from cover to cover in bookshops. I don't buy the ones that I feel have shown me everything that there is to see. Why would I?

Rhythm

Rhythm and rhyme are often spoken about in one breath. This is a mistake when talking about picture-book texts. *All* good picture books need a good, read-aloud rhythm; only a few directly use rhyme. Alliteration also falls into the rhythm camp.

Emily Gravett gets every possible rhythmic permutation out of her five words: 'apple, pear; orange bear; apple, orange, pear bear'. She uses one word, then two, then three, then four, sometimes with commas and sometimes without, and then heads back the way she has come to end on one word again. This variety gives the reader something to latch on to, which, with just five words, is especially important. *Something Else* opens with four lines, all of different lengths: 'On a windy hill / alone / with nothing to be friends with / lived Something Else.' Again, the reader has a chance to weight the words differently every time the book is read.

All the authors in my list of examples avoid sentences of the same length and shape. Even Ian Beck mixes it up a little, every now and again giving us one word on a double-page spread, or two on a single image. Rhythm is an essential part of any good writing, but it is especially important when the text is designed to be read aloud.

Rhyme

Julia Donaldson is well known for her rhyming texts, but she has a background in songwriting for children and therefore understands rhyme better than most of us. Generally speaking, rhyme is a tough area for a first-time writer. There are no short cuts, no handy tricks. Your vocabulary and grammar are strictly limited. Have you ever tried rhyming 'orange'? Additionally, publishers don't like rhyme because it is often hard to translate. And, as described above, the translation market is crucial for the success of a picture book, whose full-colour pages are extremely expensive to produce.

However, all is not doom and gloom. The occasional rhyming word can work very well. Emily Gravett adds a lovely extra layer by using 'there' at the end of *Orange Pear Apple Bear*. And if you're good, you could end up very well loved indeed.

REPETITION

Repetition ties in with rhythm. Children at this age enjoy repeated words and phrases when they are carefully used. They remember them, they anticipate them, they sometimes shout them out before you get there.

'The boy had caught a star. A star of his very own,' declares the last page of *How to Catch a Star*. The repetition of 'a star' slows the text down, bringing it gently to a stop, rather like applying the brakes on a car.

Workshop

For this chapter's workshop I'm going to ask you to use a 32-page layout, like the one we looked at in the case study, to sketch out the bones of a well-known fairy tale, 'Red Riding Hood'. I'm not looking for originality in storytelling here. The idea is to get you used to the discipline of working within a tight format. Just note down on each double-page spread what part of the story you are trying to get across, whether that's to be in words or pictures.

Next step

In the next chapter we will look at illustrated fiction, which divides into two age brackets: young fiction (5–8) and middle-grade fiction (8–12). We will look at the four different aspects of young fiction, and the age-related divisions within middle-grade fiction.

6

Illustrated fiction

Illustrated fiction is a vast and unruly expanse of the children's market. It picks up where picture books leave off from around the age of five, although if my 12-year-old's abiding interest in Julia Donaldson is anything to go by, age limits are elastic. It officially breaks down into two distinct age brackets: **young fiction** for five- to eight-year-olds, and **middle-grade fiction** for eight- to 12-year-olds.

Young fiction subdivides a further four times into reading schemes, reading series, series fiction and chapter books across the age range. Middle-grade fiction subdivides mainly by age: eight- to ten-year-olds and ten- to 12-year-olds. There are always books that cross the divide, but the majority of books fit this pattern. It is a fun, wide-ranging area for which to write and illustrate.

The illustrations

First, a note on the illustrations typically found in illustrated fiction (with some notable exceptions such as reading series – see below). Unlike picture books, the vast majority of illustrations in young and middle-grade fiction are black and white. There are two types of black-and-white illustration – **line** and **tone**:

- Line drawings very much do what they say: a hard black line on a white background. Shade and shadow are suggested by lines drawn closer together or further apart, sometimes crosshatched. All the lines, regardless of effect, are the same deep black. Great line artists in children's books at the moment include Chris Riddell and David Tazzyman; Arthur Rackham and Edward Ardizzone flew the flag in the past.

- Tone drawings offer much subtler differences, shading all the way from deep black to palest grey. These different shades require greyscale printing, as when you print a colour image using your black-and-white printer at home. Images are often generated digitally, or by hand in pen-and-wash or watercolour. Black-and-white tone illustrations are rarer than black-and-white line.

Young fiction

Alison Stanley, Writers' & Artists' Yearbook 2010

'The anticipation in excitedly turning over the page to find out what happens next; the thrill of a guessed word being right; and the beginning of reading for pleasure are all magical moments to witness.'

Young fiction is where the relationship between words and pictures begins to change. The crucial difference between these books and the picture books that precede them is that you are now talking directly to the children themselves, and not through an intermediary figure like a parent or a teacher. Illustrations still play an important part in the storytelling, but design and layout are less interesting, with more emphasis placed on strong stories and word count.

There is plenty of variety within this area. Young fiction as a whole focuses on children aged five to eight, roughly corresponding with the UK primary-school years of Reception to Year 4 (in the US, Kindergarten to Grade 3). Word count ranges from 1,000 words (picking up where picture books leave off) to as many as 15,000. Illustrations vary from full-colour for reading schemes and reading series, through to black and white for series fiction and chapter books. There is plenty of overlap with picture books, but the format is different: the books are all neater and smaller, designed for children's hands rather than adult ones.

There are lots of different names for these different areas of young fiction, and a fair degree of overlap among them as well. It can be confusing, but bear with me and I'll try to guide you through the maze.

Before we look at the most exciting and creative types of illustrated fiction, it would be useful to look at those categories that are important but less likely to yield publishing opportunities: reading schemes and reading series.

READING SCHEMES

These are the books most easily distinguished from the rest of the young fiction pack because they are designed for schools, to help children learn to read alongside a listening/prompting adult. This shared process is known as 'guided reading'. The text is the focus, with the pictures serving a purely functional purpose: to illustrate the meaning of the words and build a child's vocabulary. The books tend to look functional as well, often stapled through the middle and with none of the sparkly, shiny effects associated with titles trying to catch your eye in mainstream bookshops. Reading schemes start from ground zero: the point where a child has no concept of reading words at all.

The best-known books of this type in the UK are probably the Oxford Reading Tree books, published by Oxford University Press. If you live in the UK and have children, these books starring siblings Biff, Chip and Kipper will be familiar from your children's school bags. First published 30 years ago, the Biff and Chip stories now run into the hundreds, with language, structure and content graded according to 11 different colour-coded levels of age and ability.

You can sometimes find reading schemes on the shelves of your local library or bookshop, but you will find a better selection by trawling through the shelves at your local primary school.

Reading schemes are aimed at an international market, selling to schools in English-speaking countries all over the world. This won't surprise you if you've read the chapter on picture books and grasped the expense of four-colour printing and the consequent importance of international sales.

Key idea

Reading schemes are always produced by education professionals. If this area interests you, make sure that you have some educational or teaching experience.

Unless you are already well established in the industry, reading schemes are about *other people's* ideas, with editors controlling content, word count, illustration style and subject matter. It's never about the author or illustrator, but about the scheme: Pearson's Bug Club, to take another example, or Collins's Big Cat. If you don't enjoy taking direction and want to write and draw your own material, reading schemes probably aren't for you.

Write/draw

Take a look at the lines below. They are based on the reading-scheme book *The Magic Key* by Roderick Hunt and Alex Brychta (Level 5, Oxford Reading Tree), but with some content amended. Which words, expressions and sentence constructions do you think a five-year-old child would struggle with?

Biff and Chip gawped at the box covered in red swirly patterns.

There was something inside, glowing as brightly as a meteor.

No sooner had they opened it than they were peering inside.

'Wowsers,' Biff yelped in astonishment. 'That is some crazy magic.'

How would you simplify this for a child just learning to read? Illustrate the text if you want. Remember to share the burden of information between the words and the pictures. The correct text (as published) is at the end of this chapter for you to check against your answer.

READING SERIES

Reading series are the fuzziest of the young fiction areas to define. They are variously known as reading series, series reads, first readers, early readers, picture storybooks and other similar combinations. Whatever you call them – and I will call them 'reading series' for purposes of consistency here – they are considered the 'fun' side of literacy. They have fewer rules and regulations than reading schemes, but they still work as tools to help children learn to read. They are roughly banded according to ability, although not to the same degree as reading schemes.

Reading series are designed for independent reading, but are often used for guided reading in schools as well. They are generally printed in full colour, so the usual rules apply about ideas needing international appeal. They have more room to play around than reading schemes do, so you will sometimes find Internet links and puzzles relating to the material scattered through the books.

Reading series often use well-known names. Established authors like Anne Fine and Michael Morpurgo have worked for the Egmont reading series Bananas, as have illustrators such as Korky Paul and Liz Pichon. However, it's not the big names that sell the books so much as the brand, and the sense of the books being part of a collectable, matching series that will decorate a bookshelf.

These books are short, so make very little visual impact in a bookshop when shelved with their narrow spines facing out. As such, the unified look of the series brand is what keeps these titles visible for buyers. The concept of a 'series' here doesn't mean interconnected stories. Interconnected stories are the meat and drink of the next area I want to talk to you about: series fiction.

SERIES FICTION

Now we are getting to the fun stuff: the place of opportunity for aspiring writers. Series fiction is a fantastic springboard into the world of writing for anyone, regardless of experience.

Once upon a time, a group of editors sat around a table, brainstorming ideas for a new children's series for girls aged between six and nine. It needed to be collectable with a strong series identity. One editor put up her hand. 'I had an idea for a series when I was seven years old,' she said. 'It was about seven fairies. One for each colour of the rainbow.'

The series, Rainbow Magic, by Daisy Meadows, has since spawned over 200 titles. There are mini-series of four or seven interconnected titles within the overarching series that share common themes: the rainbow, the weather, the ocean, pop stars and animals to give a few examples. Sales of the series currently stand at over 10 million copies worldwide.

You might assume, on those statistics, that Rainbow Magic has made its author rich. It has, but not in the way you might imagine. It was an *editor's* idea. Daisy Meadows doesn't exist. She is an amalgam of dozens of different writers and editors, all of whom have taken a share of her profits. She is successful because she is the product of professional, dedicated teams who know how to produce books that children love. The same is true of Lucy Daniels – whose Animal Ark series could be said to have started the whole series fiction phenomenon in the 1990s – and Adam Blade, more recent 'author' of the Beast Quest series. There are plenty of other examples, but these are perhaps the best known.

When people first learn this, they are often surprised and baffled. What is the point? they want to know. Why do publishers produce books in this way? Shouldn't they be supporting original talent, promoting real authors?

The point is that a fictional author has no rights over a series, so that series is more flexible and profitable for a publisher or a packager (more on packagers in a moment). A fictional author can also 'write' six or more books at the same time, which does wonders for a publisher's production line and – you've guessed it – profits. A fictional author can be designed to fit a niche in the market. They can be given an alphabetically appropriate name to meet a browser's eye level, or queue-barge on to the shelf before the direct competition. They can be designed to fit as many commercial platforms as possible should opportunity present: clothing, online games, stationery. They can also enjoy lives far more exotic than those of real authors, giving publicity departments lots of material to work with. I'm always amused by Adam Blade's biography, which gives him a pet capuchin monkey named Omar.

If this seems hard-nosed and commercial, it is. Publishing is a business, and it has to think like a business in order to survive, particularly in the current climate where books fight to be heard above the clamour of video games and all the other distractions modern children contend with. And as if the competition weren't tough enough, publishing is an industry with very low margins. A book is cheap compared to a games console; it's cheap compared to a pair of decent socks. In order to turn a profit these days, publishers need to sell a *lot* of books. A title ideally needs to shift around ten thousand copies a year, more if it's an expensive full-colour book.

Adam Blade, Daisy Meadows and friends sell in these quantities. Their success bankrolls the quieter titles, the books that publishers love but which won't set a financial spreadsheet alight: the stand-alones, the ones with sad endings and quirky illustrations and unusual production values, the literary prize-winners and the poetry and all the things that keep a publishing list energized and wide-ranging.

There are dozens of well-known authors now established in their own right who have written packaged series fiction at some point in their careers. Advances aren't high, but the steady stream of royalties often means that the projects are worth while. It is a dependable source of income in an unreliable industry. Or 'gas-bill money', as literary agent Lesley Hadcroft once put it.

Publishers are wise to the series-fiction juggernaut and regularly design their own series, commissioning authors and illustrators without the trouble and expense of the middleman. But, on the whole, series fiction originates with packagers.

 Hothouse Fiction website (www.hothousefiction.com)

'From the seed of an original idea, we develop characters, settings and plots, and then collaborate with talented writers to turn our concepts into proposals for full book series, which are then presented to publishers.'

Packagers are an intermediary business. They produce ideas and source writers. But they still have to pitch those ideas to publishers for publication and distribution. In that respect, they are in the same boat as the solo author rapping on doors to get a commissioning editor's attention. However, publishers take packagers with good track records more seriously than they might a first-time author. Working Partners, for example, has produced some of the biggest series in recent years, including Rainbow Magic and Beast Quest, while Hothouse Fiction has Secret Kingdom in its stable, among others.

Packagers employ teams of highly experienced editors who have regular meetings to exchange ideas for series, like the meeting described in the opening paragraph of this section. When an idea has been agreed, they will either find a publisher to take it on the strength of the idea (a rare Holy Grail) or, more often, they will ask writers to produce some sample material to fit the concept before presenting it to publishers. The writer is given character names, scenes and complete chapter breakdowns by the packager, with express instructions to 'colour them in': fill out the characters, develop the scenes, make the language as exciting as possible. There is no fee for sample material, but writers are usually happy to oblige in the knowledge that a little free work can sometimes net a paid project. In terms of cold hard cash, there is usually a small advance if the project is accepted, with around one-third of the royalty charged by the packagers going to the writer.

Packagers actively recruit writers. Go to the Working Partners or Hothouse Fiction websites and it's hard to miss the great big button shouting APPLY NOW! There are forms to fill in regarding experience and interests, and you are asked to submit some sample writing.

You will note that packagers are all about the *writer*. Illustration and design for this type of series fiction lies strictly with the publisher who buys the concept. If you are an illustrator or author-illustrator, the packaging route isn't for you. If you are a writer: hello, opportunity!

CHAPTER BOOKS

And, finally, we reach the area of young fiction that you have probably been envisaging all along. Chapter books do what they say: they tell stories broken into chapters. For children new to reading, chapters are crucial to mark their progress. Chapters bring them a step closer to books for older children/young adults; chapters teach them to anticipate what lies ahead. Chapters break a daunting story of 10,000 words into much more manageable chunks of 1,000–1,500 words, and contain mini-narrative arcs all of their own: beginnings, middles and those all-important cliffhanger ends.

This area is where you'll find what's known as author-led fiction: books produced by 'real' authors and illustrators in their own distinctive styles. Strong, identifiable characters are key for this age range, over and above zany plots and exotic settings. Francesca Simon's Horrid Henry series demonstrates this beautifully. The majority of these books feature black-and-white illustrations, although there are exceptions out there at the moment experimenting with two- and three-colour printing: Alex T. Smith's Claude books for one, and Shirley Hughes and Claire Vulliamy's Dixie O'Day series. (It's interesting to note that all three of the books I mention above use the main character's name in their titles.) With fewer colours used in the printing process, these books are cheaper to produce, and so can take a few more risks: these are the titles where you're more likely to find the quirky humour, odd vocabulary, unusual author-illustrator collaborations and unexpected design.

Most author-led chapter books in young fiction develop into series, with stand-alone titles almost unheard of for the same reason I gave when talking about reading series: visibility. It's a tough area for new writers and illustrators to break into, but who knows? With practice, you could be one of the lucky ones.

Structuring a young fiction book

Layout for young fiction isn't as restrictive as it is for picture books. However, there are still rules that you want to be aware of.

Word count varies widely, from a few hundred words for reading-scheme books to as many as 15,000 words for chapter books. Page count rarely goes above 128 pages – which, you will note, is neatly divisible by 8, to fit the multiples-of-8 principle of printing presses at a minimum cost. If a story falls short of these ideal word/page counts, publishers are adept at filling the blank pages with ads and teasers.

Reading-scheme books for beginners don't tend to have chapters. Learning to sustain focus from chapter to chapter is a skill that develops later. Reading-scheme books for older, more capable readers can have four or five chapters, sometimes only 200–300 words long, with plenty of illustrations to aid comprehension. Reading series and chapter books can sometimes feature three loosely connected short stories, as in Joanna Nadin's Penny Dreadful books, which don't overly tax a young reader's concentration. Individual titles in series fiction like Beast Quest are approximately 10,000 words in length, divided into ten chapters of 1,000 words each, variable by a couple of hundred words in either direction. Finally, longer chapter books may have up to 15,000 words, but the chapter length will still be around 1,000–1,250 words. Pictures at this level are most often black and white, with around 40 illustrations per book – roughly four per chapter.

Snapshot

Visit your bookshop or library and take a look at four books classified as young fiction. Estimate the word count. Are the pages divisible by 8? Do they feature chapters? Are the illustrations black and white? Are they line or tone? Estimate how many illustrations. Has the publisher filled the end of the book with ads and teasers for other books?

Case study: *Penguins: Star Attack!* by Lucy Courtenay

Let's take a look at a chapter breakdown for my series fiction book *Space Penguins: Star Attack!*, aimed at six- to eight-year-olds with some overspill of interest for eight- to ten-year-olds (I told you these things cross divides). It is around 10,000 words long with a 112-page extent (yes, divisible by 8 again). It features a prologue, ten chapters and an epilogue.

Prologue: ICEcube, the Space Penguins' intergalactic computer engine, gives a little background on the Space Penguins, describing the characters and setting the scene for what is about to happen.

Chapter 1: A pizza delivery astronaut is sucked into the tractor beam of a vast space station. Before he disappears, he sends a mayday message to the Space Penguins.

Chapter 2: The Space Penguins are going about their normal(ish) business when the pizza delivery astronaut's message comes through. Space Penguins to the rescue!

Chapter 3: The Space Penguins are also gobbled up by the space station's tractor beam. They are confronted by an army of robot seals.

Chapter 4: The Space Penguins fight the robot seals but are captured. They meet their old enemy, Dark Wader.

Chapter 5: Dark Wader appears to be nice to the Space Penguins. In reality, he is spying on them. He has a plan...

Chapter 6: The Space Penguins trick Dark Wader into revealing where he is keeping the pizza delivery astronaut.

Chapter 7: Dark Wader wants the Space Penguins to stay with him as he rules the universe. The Space Penguins say no. They are taken to the jail cells.

Chapter 8: They meet the pizza delivery astronaut in the jail cells. They escape together, but one of the crew – Fuzz – is captured.

Chapter 9: In the final battle to rescue Fuzz, Dark Wader uses a robot killer whale. HOW WILL THE SPACE PENGUINS GET OUT OF THIS ONE?

Chapter 10: The Space Penguins turn off the gravity on the space station and escape, taking the pizza delivery boy with them. Dark Wader is furious.

Epilogue: Dark Wader watches them leave. He has left a spying device on the Space Penguins' ship. He looks forward to seeing them again very soon...

There are eight books in the series, and they all break down in a similar way: a prologue to set the scene; Chapters 1–2 to set up the problem; Chapters 3–8 to ratchet up the drama as the Space Penguins lurch from one situation to the next, sometimes winning and sometimes not; Chapter 9 to bring the story to a climax; and Chapter 10 where all is resolved, with a twist revealed in the epilogue. If you were to visualize this narrative arc on a graph, it would take off sharply, dip and rise through the middle, peak at Chapter 9 and tail away with a satisfied sigh at the end.

The illustrations, by James Davies, also follow a pattern. There are around ten double-page spreads (illustrations that stretch over two pages) including one that repeats in every book: a spread of stats on the five penguin characters at the beginning. There are then five full-page illustrations, with the rest an assortment of half- and quarter-page illustrations varied through the text. The big pictures are reserved for the big moments: the appearance of the robot killer whale, the zero-gravity battle, a menacing rear view of Dark Wader watching the Space Penguins escaping. The smaller pictures give flashes of character, showcase minor aspects of the story and highlight jokes.

This structure isn't fixed in concrete for all young fiction. But it works for these stories, and is as good a starting point for illustrated series fiction as any. When you reach the chapter on plotting (Chapter 8), you should find yourself building your young fiction in a similar way.

Common ground

With four such different aspects of young fiction to think about, it's easy to feel lost when considering writing for this age group. Don't worry about it. The books all come down to the same thing: a well-told story at an appropriate level, a structured plot, a strong narrative arc, good characters and an interesting setting, supported throughout by illustrations. The main question to ask is this. Are you desperate to write and/or illustrate your own fantastic idea, or are you simply desperate to write and/or illustrate? If you are determined to make your own way, chapter books are probably your best bet, but don't dismiss the other areas as good starting points. I wrote series fiction for several years before producing my own work. I would say: get as much experience in as many directions as you can.

Snapshot

Which of the following sounds most like you?

1   You have a fully formed idea about a tightrope-walking ant that you have written and illustrated yourself.

2   You know a lot about horses and would love a chance to write stories about them, but you don't know where to start.

3   You are a primary-school teacher keen to develop something to help reluctant readers.

4   You have a degree in illustration and a strong desire to illustrate children's books.

5   You have written a story and your friend has illustrated it.

If you fit 1, the subject matter sounds better suited to picture books than illustrated fiction. And you might like to think about what I said in the previous chapter about illustrating your own stories. However, if you feel that the writing has a greater part to play than the pictures, chapter books are probably the right area for you. Put your pictures aside for now and focus on your story.

If you fit 2, you might like to think about writing for a packager. Horses sell well, as do many animals. Take a look at packager websites such as Working Partners and Hothouse Fiction and follow instructions on how to apply to write for them.

If 3 is your area, apply to reading-scheme publishers with a letter outlining your experience and your ideas. Don't send material you have already written. There is only the slimmest of chances that it will match what the publisher is looking for. It's far better to have a conversation first.

If you are 4, send material (*never* originals) to illustration agents, outlining the type of work you would like to do. Get your pictures on to relevant websites. Don't approach publishers directly; your chances of catching an art director's eye at a publishing house are slimmer than a sausage finding a fan at a vegetarian convention. If you're good, you will be taken on by an agent and work will, with any luck, follow.

If 5 is you, congratulations on finishing a story! I hope you and your friend enjoyed creating it. If you want to see your book published, however, I politely refer you again to the previous chapter, about illustrating work before submitting it. If your friend doesn't have at least a degree in illustration, you will struggle to place your work. Publishers like to choose their own illustrators for texts, and sending them material that has already been illustrated can halve your chances of being accepted. You and your friend would be better to approach separate agents: one for text, one for illustration. And then who knows? You may work together in the end.

Middle-grade fiction

Middle-grade fiction is an expression originating in the United States, but widely understood in the UK market. It covers that classic territory of children's books, those aimed at eight- to 12-year-olds.

As we established in an earlier chapter, children and their reading interests change quickly. A child develops enormously between the ages of eight and 12, with the age straddling that unimaginably huge leap from primary to secondary school and all the experiences that go with it. It makes no sense for publishers or writers to bracket eight- to 12-year-olds together other than in the most general terms, so middle-grade fiction is usually subdivided by age: eight- to ten-year-olds and ten- to 12-year-olds.

Eight- to ten-year-olds are still very young, with their primary schools and home environments still very much their main influences. Books about school and family life work well for this age group, with a heavy emphasis on strong, identifiable characters as outlined above. Word count rarely goes above 30,000. There has been enormous success for school- and family-led books with heavily integrated illustrations for this age range in recent years, such as Liz Pichon's doodle-heavy Tom Gates series and Jeff Kinney's *Diary of a Wimpy Kid*. Visual interest on every page has been the key to these books' success. It is more important than ever in the fast-moving world of the twenty-first century that books for eight- to ten-year-olds keep a reader's eyes as stimulated and entertained as their brains.

Ten- to 12-year-olds are moving into a more text-heavy environment, with books sometimes ratcheting the word count up into the hundreds of thousands. These books often feature illustrations as chapter heads (small images at the head of each chapter) only, if at all. In some books, each chapter head is different; in others, three or four chapter heads might alternate. Chapter length stands at around 1,500–2,000 words, and books can stretch to 40 or more chapters. The number of illustrations is determined by budget. Heavily illustrated, full-colour middle-grade fiction – vastly expensive – is reserved for the established heavyweights of the trade such as The Chronicles of Narnia and *Alice's Adventures in Wonderland*.

When writing for this age range, there has always been a sense that there is less need to focus on how the story will work visually. But who is to say that fiction for ten- to 12-year-olds won't move in the same visual direction as fiction for eight- to 10-year-olds? If the increasing pace of life beyond school and home is any indication, this may well be the next niche in the market.

Workshop

This time I want you to take a children's film of your choice (it will clearly need to be quite a meaty one) and plan a chapter book around it. Aim for ten chapters. Write down briefly what happens in each chapter, plus the major illustrations you would like to see included – which should be used to help establish the setting and the characters, for the big moments and so on.

Next step

In the next chapter we will look at the importance of character in children's books. We will consider ages, visual and personality quirks, and the importance of developing both interior and exterior worlds for your characters. We will also look at secondary characters, the use of dialogue, and explore the rules of 'Show, don't tell' in characterization.

Write: answer

Biff and Chip looked at the box.

Something was glowing inside it.

They opened the box. They looked inside.

'It's magic,' they said.

Source: *The Magic Key* (Level 5 Oxford Reading Tree) by Roderick Hunt and Alex Brychta

7

Character

It seems like an obvious point to make, but the root of all successful stories lies with *character*, far away and above exciting plotlines, intense emotion or crazy action. You can have the most heart-pumping story ever devised but, if the characters enacting the drama are flat, then the story will fail. Nowhere does this hold truer than in children's books.

 Ray Bradbury, *Zen in the Art of Writing*

'Plot is no more than footprints left in the snow after your characters have run by on their way to incredible destinations.'

The importance of *people*, human or otherwise

Let's get one thing out of the way before we begin. Adults may be able to read books about landscape and architecture, but children struggle to follow books about inanimate objects. For this very reason, I urge you to put away any thoughts you are having about creating books about Trevor the Telegraph Pole, Stanley the Scooter or Padma the Potato. Your role as storyteller may lie in breathing life into characters, but your characters should already be breathing by themselves to some degree. Yes, Thomas the Tank Engine was inanimate – but Thomas was originally published in 1946, and the past, as L. P. Hartley once said, is a foreign country.

Children build their knowledge and understanding of the world through *people*. Every day, lessons are learned among, with and against those people: parents, siblings, teachers, friends and enemies. For people you can probably read pets, too. Every living creature in that child's life is a character in the great manuscript of their lives.

A vast number of titles for young children feature the main character's name: Penny Dreadful, Horrid Henry, Harry Potter, Mr Gum, Tom Gates… The sheer quantity of books that do this illustrates this importance of character for this age group. Building a great character is something all writers and illustrators should try to do before fleshing out an idea into a plot. Get your character right, and your plot might even write itself.

We've spent several chapters at the beginning of this book looking at how to generate ideas, yet now I appear to be telling you that characters are more important than anything else? Don't feel puzzled or annoyed by this. Everything you have done so far is vital context, groundwork, preparation of the canvas. But I can't stress enough that, in any story for children at this level, what happens is nowhere near as important as who it happens *to*.

Ernest Hemingway, *Death in the Afternoon*

'*When writing a novel a writer should create living people; people not characters. A character is a caricature.*'

Hemingway's advice on creating characters may be relevant to novel writing, but I'm inclined to throw it out of the window when advising on developing characters for children's books. Of course, your characters should have real aspects and recognizable elements, or your readers won't be interested in them. But in children's books characters *can* be exaggerated into caricatures. For young readers I would even say they *must* be exaggerated.

A useful phrase to bear in mind when you create characters for children's books is 'bold lines'. Grey areas and middle ground don't work for this age group. Characters in children's books need to be bigger and better than in real life. If your character is loud, make them really loud. If they are quiet and gentle, ensure that they are the gentlest, quietest creatures around. A great character in illustrated fiction needs to leap off the page and sear itself into a young reader's mind. It can't take an average line.

Just a number

It's important to get the age of your main character right. Children's book characters are almost always children themselves, whether in human, animal or alien form. They have recognizable childlike characteristics and childish concerns. Children aren't interested in adults, on the whole. They have no concept of what it will be like to be a grown-up, and no real desire to find out. Roald Dahl bucked the trend with his book *Esio Trot* about two pensioners falling in love, but he was Roald Dahl.

Children aren't interested in reading about children younger than themselves either. It is beneath them. They aren't even very interested in reading about children the same age. You should aim to keep your characters around two years older than your readers. Bring to mind the way a child will always hurry after his or her older siblings, keen to play their games and emulate their ways and grow up to be just like them. When you're eight, the prospect of being ten – double figures! – is extremely alluring. Horrid Henry is about ten years old, where the average Horrid Henry reader's age is probably seven or eight. Charlie Bucket likewise. Peppa Pig is somewhere around five or six, with the vast majority of her audience three to four years old.

Focus point

In short: for picture books your character should be about six. For young fiction, keep them between eight and ten; for middle-grade fiction, between ten and 14. You don't have to be too literal about it – we don't need to know that Wonky the Wallaby is precisely six years old – but do bear in mind age-appropriate interests and behaviour.

Other ages can, do and should feature in illustrated children's books. Tom Gates's sister Delia in her dark glasses is a teenager; Manny is Greg Heffley's baby brother in *Diary of a Wimpy Kid*. But ten-year-old Tom and 12-year-old Greg are the characters your readers will be rooting for.

Physical versus personal

There are two things to consider when developing characters:

1 the physical aspect
2 personality.

In other words, consider what they look like and how they behave. The boy in the wolfsuit, the patchwork elephant and the boy who loves stars – taken from Maurice Sendak's *Where the Wild Things Are*, *Elmer* by David McKee and *How to Catch a Star* by Oliver Jeffers – are captured with emotional as well as physical detail: the boy in the wolfsuit is angry, the elephant is cheerful, the boy who loves stars is lonely. The challenge in illustrated fiction lies in striking the balance, judging how much of each element to leave to the pictures and how much to the words. It can be a mistake to spend too much time describing someone's looks and personality in detail where a picture will say the same thing more briefly and colourfully. Equally, avoiding physical or emotional description altogether can lay too much responsibility for characterization on the pictures, and leave the text feeling either too weak or redundant altogether. You must judge where to stand on that particular seesaw.

Although a character's physical appearance can be interesting, it will rarely be the driving force behind a story. So, first of all, I would advise you to resist the temptation to describe verbally every curl on your character's head or freckle on their face. Most physical aspects will fall to the illustrator, not the writer. If you *are* the illustrator, save most of the physical details for your sketches, and not for the text.

Given the importance of the international market for full-colour picture books, you will also have to consider the cultural implications of physical description. Hair and eye colours and minutely observed skin tones won't necessarily translate in other countries and cultures. Human faces vary hugely from one place to the next, and it is very difficult for illustrators of one culture to draw human characteristics from another with accuracy. I remember once working on a new cover for Beverley Naidoo's classic book *Journey to Jo'burg*, and having an awkward conversation with her about how the children on the new cover did *not* have South African faces, and had the illustrator not done any research at all?

This may sound contradictory, but if you are writing a character (as opposed to illustrating one), try to approach physical description without being too physical about it. Eyes don't have to be that special shade of blue, but they can be kind or cruel or filled with tears. A nose can be snooty without getting into the specifics of bone structure and profile. Roald Dahl describes the horrible granny in *George's Marvellous Medicine* as having 'pale brown teeth and a small, puckered-up mouth like a dog's bottom'. All of these elements feed far more powerfully into the creation of character than red curly hair or a dimple in one cheek.

The revolting physical descriptions of Roald Dahl's Mr Twit perfectly match his even more horrible personality:

> 'Mr Twit didn't even bother to open his mouth wide when he ate. As a result (and because he never washed) there were always hundreds of bits of old breakfasts and lunches and suppers sticking to the hairs around his face … What I'm trying to tell you is that Mr Twit was a foul and smelly old man. He was also an extremely horrid old man, as you will find out in a moment.'

Roald Dahl takes a more emotional, behavioural angle on Mrs Twit's character than he does with Mr Twit. This is probably because, having established Mr Twit so physically, Dahl instinctively knew that approaching Mrs Twit in the same way would be boring and repetitive. Her ugliness is therefore attributed to ugly thoughts:

> 'If a person has ugly thoughts, it begins to show on the face. And when that person has ugly thoughts every day, every week, every year, the face gets uglier and uglier until it gets so ugly you can hardly bear to look at it. A person who has good thoughts cannot ever be ugly. You can have a wonky nose and a crooked mouth and a double chin and stick-out teeth, but if you have good thoughts they will shine out of your face like sunbeams and you will always look lovely.'

Cressida Cowell, who illustrates as well as writes the *How to Train Your Dragon* series, has a useful take on how to write about a character's physical attributes. Stoick the Vast, Chieftain of the Hooligan Tribe, is described as having a big, wild beard. So far, so physical. But then she plays around with the beard's visual potential by using similes.

A simile, in case you have forgotten your English lessons at school, is 'a figure of speech involving the comparison of one thing with another thing of a different kind' (*Concise Oxford Dictionary*), and is used to make a description more vivid, for example 'as brave as a lion' and 'as fit as a flea'.

While I want you to commit this definition to mind, I also command you to forget the examples instantly. If you use them in your writing, you are committing the crime of cliché, an offence more closely examined later in this book. It's far better to play around with surprising alternatives. In *How to Twist a Dragon's Tale*, Cressida describes Stoick as having 'a beard like an electrocuted Afghan hound'. In *A Hero's Guide to Deadly Dragons*, it's 'a beard like a hedgehog struck by lightning'. The unexpected images these similes conjure are so bright and clear that the beard almost becomes a character in its own right.

Metaphors, for the sake of clarity, don't use 'like' or 'as' when they describe things. They get closer to the action. Shakespeare's 'All the world's a stage' is a famous example of a metaphor at work. With a metaphor, Stoick's beard would BE an electrocuted Afghan hound.

Write/draw

- Look at yourself in a mirror.
- Describe the following physical aspects of yourself: eyes/lips/ears/nose/hair. For example: My eyes are green.
- Now give them an emotional attribute. For example: My eyes are green and sad.
- Now add a visual simile. Make it as unexpected as you can; you may be surprised by the effect. For example: My eyes are green and as sad as a cat in the rain.

If you are an artist, do the same exercise by drawing the physical, emotional and descriptive elements. Then send me a copy of any eyes resembling cats in the rain via the publisher (address at the beginning of this book). This I have to see.

Expect the unexpected

Of course, you don't have to do what it says on the tin. Instead of using physical description to reinforce a character, you can invert expectations instead, where a character might look one way and act another. For example, Ed Vere's Mr Big is a huge gorilla that terrifies everyone with his size, where in fact he is gentle and lonely with a hidden talent for playing jazz piano. This contradiction between appearance and personality can have double the impact if you play it right. But it can also confuse, with the opposing characteristics cancelling each other out and leaving you with nothing, so it's important to weight each aspect carefully.

Interior world

To get to know your character, try to build a clear picture of their *interior* as well as their exterior world. What do they like and dislike? Who do they love above all others, and who do they hate? What relationship do they have with their parents? Are they gregarious or solitary? Ambitious or shy – or, indeed, shyly ambitious? Malorie Blackman, the UK's Children's Laureate from 2013 to 2015, is well known for working out her characters to this level before she plots. She devotes so much attention to developing their personalities that she begins to know how they would act in any given situation, opening the door to all kinds of ideas. Quentin Blake, when developing his wordless picture book *Clown*, spent a great deal of time getting to know his little clown before he looked at how to put the rest of the story together. J. K. Rowling filled pages of notebooks with background information on characters; she even knew who among her minor characters would marry whom 20 years into the future. My own Naughty Fairies series for Hodder revolved around six distinct fairy personalities – a grumpy one, an boastful one, an animal-loving one and so on – all carefully developed before I touched on any plots. Within a couple of books, the characters were dictating the direction of the stories.

Even if 90 per cent of the information you amass in this way never makes it on to the page, it will still make your character more believable to readers because *you* know them inside out. It shows.

Write

Find an image of a person that interests you. This could be a family member or a celebrity from a magazine, a random newspaper photograph, a painted portrait – anything human. Study it closely.

- Note as many physical aspects as you can: hair, eye colour, shape of nose and mouth and ears. Are they fat or thin? Tall or short? Don't worry about describing their clothes; this is about the person.

- Now study the picture from an emotional angle. Do they look kind or cruel? Happy or unhappy? Scared, excited, furious? What is it about their physical features that suggests these emotions?
- Now write five sentences describing this person's physical characteristics via the emotions that they convey. For example: she has kind eyes. Add similes for effect.

Develop this exercise further by building an interior world for them as well.

Human or animal?

Animal stories are dominant in picture books because of the international aspect. To sell a book to 15 different countries, you need a character that all your readers will recognize and respond to. A British street urchin living on the docks would struggle to sell internationally because the child's features, skin colour, clothes and so on would be unfamiliar beyond UK borders. (Remember an earlier point I made about avoiding anything local or specific to a region if you want to find a publisher.) A British street *cat* living on the same docks, on the other hand, could work in every country that has ever seen a cat or a ship. It could be exactly the same story, but the cat would sell where the boy wouldn't.

It's far better, then, to approach a children's book character as an animal. Whether you are from Denmark, Chile or Laos, the chances are that you know what a lion is, or an elephant, or a rabbit. Certain animals don't translate – hedgehogs, for example, are tricky outside the UK, and pigs come with a raft of religious issues and are best avoided. Being British, I've always struggled with raccoons. But, chosen wisely, animals neatly bypass most problems of cross-cultural referencing.

Western culture in particular enjoys anthropomorphizing animals, attributing human emotions to the pet cat or the elderly camel at the safari park. Countless videos attest to our never-ending amusement with the idea that animals think like we do. Animals share a lot of childlike characteristics: big eyes, fat tummies, cuteness, and a body often proportionally larger in relation to its limbs. They are also very straightforward in their needs – for food, sleep and so forth – which aligns neatly with the simple plotting needed for young children. And illustrators prefer drawing animals anyway because they are, on the whole, easier than humans.

There is the additional advantage of *distance* when telling a story with animal characters. Tell a little girl a tale about another little girl wandering through a dark forest with dangerous creatures trying to eat her, and you could make your listener identify a little too closely with the character's peril. Tell a girl the same story about a mouse, and you have *The Gruffalo*.

The proportion of animal characters lessens as you move into older, black-and-white illustrated fiction. Animals still feature, but they aren't so frequently anthropomorphized. Instead, they are allowed to be real animals in real environments: pet cats and dogs and hamsters, penguins at the zoo, wild ponies on holiday, mice in the attic and so on. This may be because the international market isn't so crucial for a book's profit margins, allowing authors to experiment more widely with human characters tied to specific environments. Older children also have more emotional resilience, and can relate to characters' dilemmas with less need of an animal avatar to take the blows.

There *are* animal characters out there beyond young middle-grade fiction (8–10) but they are hard to find. The only such books starring anthropomorphized animal characters that come to mind are titles from a time when publishing was a very different (ehem) animal: the rabbits of *Watership Down* by Richard Adams (1977), the moles of William Horwood's *Duncton Wood* (1980) (a book not specifically aimed at children) and the Redwall series by Brian Jacques (1986 onwards).

Snapshot

Study a picture of an animal in the same way as you studied the picture of a person in the earlier exercise. Are there any physical aspects of the animal that suggest its personality? For example, a roaring lion = angry.

Secondary characters

Victoria Turnbull, author-illustrator of *The Sea Tiger*

'Most of my research for the book involved drawing the two main characters over and over again in order to get to know them and explore their relationship with each other. The story developed from these character sketches.'

There are books for very young children that focus on just one well-drawn character, such as Mick Inkpen's Kipper books. The plots revolve entirely around one solitary character and the immediate problems in its life. They can work well if that character is strong enough to hold an entire story arc without any assistance. But I think the fun really begins when you have two or more characters to play with – particularly if your second character stands in direct conflict with your first.

Take Francesca Simon's Horrid Henry, a character neatly summarized by his name. Give him an angelic brother called Perfect Peter. Throw the two boys in a room, lock the door and watch through the keyhole to see what happens next. Conflict is guaranteed. As a plot is often defined as 'what happens', by putting two characters together you start a chemical reaction that can result in a plot. This is very much what Victoria Turnbull is getting at in the quote above.

 Key idea

Plot can be generated simply by making different characters interact with each other. There is no specific need for car explosions, time-travelling beds or magical unicorn fantasy lands to make a plot come to life.

However, resist the urge for *too* many characters. No story needs a cast of hundreds. Oliver Jeffers's *The Hueys in the New*

Jumper sets one little character who dares to be different against a crowd, but this works because the crowd *is* the character, not the individuals within the mass. The same is true of Elmer and his herd of elephants. If you really want more than five or six characters, draw them clearly and keep them only where they are needed. If a character is doing nothing to further the plot, cut it out. Just as every word must earn its place on the page, so must every character.

Snapshot

Think of two animals least suited to share an enclosure in a zoo. Write down a list of their separate characteristics as far as you can. Where do you think the conflict between these animals might arise?

What do your characters want?

Horrid Henry wants to get away with all his naughty tricks and avoid school and homework for ever. Elmer the elephant wants to make people laugh, but also wants to fit in. Stoick the Vast wants his son Hiccup Horrendous Haddock III to make him proud. By giving your characters recognizable wants and desires, you put flesh on their bones. You can create characters that look and behave as oddly as you want, but they will work only if they have human motivations. Aliens? Maybe. Lost aliens who want to go home? Great, I recognize that feeling. Earthworms? Doubtful. Earthworms who want to line-dance against all the odds? Wow, let's hear it.

Take the little nameless characters in Katherine Cave and Chris Riddell's *Something Else*. They are defined by their weirdness, but also by their entirely human need to belong. By developing your characters' motivations in this way, you put them in the same boat as your human reader, allowing the reader to root for them. Obviously, certain desires are best left to fiction for older children, but even very young children understand the basics of fear, desire and anger.

Fear is often triggered by the loss or absence of something important: a parent in a supermarket aisle, or a teddy as in Shirley Hughes's *Dogger*. You will often find characters at the young end of picture books wanting to find something that they have lost, like the witch and her bow, wand and hat from Julia Donaldson and Axel Sheffler's *Room on the Broom*. Every child denied an ice cream knows about desire, making stories of wish fulfilment ever popular. Anger is Max's fuel in Maurice Sendak's *Where the Wild Things Are*. These motivations can all be used to enliven your characters and drive them through a plot.

Heroes and villains

Without shadow, light is flat. Without light, shadow is an expanse of nothing. It is the juxtaposition of the two that brings to life the shapes – the characters – you are trying to convey.

The push–pull attraction of hero/villain will always generate more energy than hero/hero or villain/villain. But remember, a villain doesn't have to be someone on the scale of Sauron or Voldemort, just as a hero doesn't have to be Frodo Baggins or Harry Potter – particularly when you are creating stories for young children. I urge you to recall my earlier advice on the importance of childishness, a child's sense of right and wrong. Remember the bitterness of falling out with friends over an obscure rule in a skipping game, or the urge for vengeance when your favourite pencil got broken? A stand-off between former friends over a disputed conker can – and should – be packed with just as much emotional charge as Saint George facing the dragon, because, to a child, *this is how it feels*.

Snapshot

Take a look at the two unlikely animals sharing that enclosure in the previous exercise.

Using the characteristics you have already listed, ask the following questions:

- What do they fear?
- What do they desire?
- What makes them angry?

Do your answers suggest any possible plots?

Show, don't tell

Anton Chekhov

'Don't tell me the moon is shining; show me the glint of light on broken glass.'

'Show, don't tell' is a phrase you may have come across in your research already. It is a golden rule in developing children's stories in matters of action, dialogue and setting as well as character. It won't be the last time I mention it, so pay close attention. It has to be the lynchpin of all you do.

So what does it mean?

When I was a teacher, I was often asked: 'Miss, how do you do this?' I would always try to answer along the lines of, 'How do you think you do it?' When children are encouraged to work answers out for themselves, their understanding will always be deeper than if you hand them the answer outright. 'Show, don't tell' means exactly this. Don't spoon-feed your readers. Make them work things out for themselves. The end result is always more complete because a reader has had to engage more deeply with the story.

When using the 'Show, don't tell' rule in developing characters, think about how you can convey a fact about your character without stating it directly. Direct statements are almost always flat and uninteresting. Take these two physical character descriptions.

Bob is a fat man.

Bob often loses the remote control in the folds of his stomach.

Which sentence has more impact? I'm staking my reputation on it being the second. (The second sentence would have more impact on an illustrator's imagination, too, which is worth bearing in mind.) You have established that Bob is fat without actually saying so. You have, instead, demonstrated his fatness. You have broadened the concept into something more interesting than a flat observation. You have *shown*, not *told*.

Now that's clear, I need to muddy the water a little. The 'Show, don't tell' approach should be used rigorously in your writing, *but not exclusively.* Sometimes you *do* need to tell, to define your boundaries and fix an initial impression that you can then build on. If you put the first and second sentences about Bob together, for example, you develop a clearer overall picture of the character than if you just use the second in isolation. Developing an instinct for when to show and when to tell comes with practice, much like a chef knowing how much salt to add to the *coq au vin*.

Write/draw

Change these 'telling' character descriptions to 'showing' ones. You can draw and/or write the result.

- Billy is very clever.
- Angus is always angry.
- Lizzy is a scaredy-cat.

Dialogue

Using dialogue for character development is more relevant to the writer than the illustrator, although word bubbles and the texture of spoken words can convey aspects of a character's personality very well. This is also very much a 'Show, don't tell' method of character development, where the words your character says and the way they say them don't just tell the reader what's happening in the plot, but offer the reader an insight into what makes the characters tick.

Here's an example, using the three characters from the previous exercise:

'Keep that r-r-r-rabbit away from m-m-me!' wept Lizzy.

'You are being ridiculous, Lizzy,' sighed Billy. 'Scientists have proved in laboratories all over the world that rabbits are harmless.'

'Don't talk to Lizzy like that!' Angus bellowed.

Nowhere in this dialogue have you said outright that Lizzy is a scaredy-cat, or that Billy is clever, or that Angus is angry. But the reader understands these aspects of their characters from the way they talk to each other.

Words like 'wept', 'sighed' and 'bellowed' are known as speech or dialogue tags. When you are developing a character, think about *how* they speak as well as what they say. Speech tags should be used with caution, however. Too many variations on 'said' will distract the eye and mind from the story you're trying to tell.

You can also 'Show, don't tell' with characters in speech by giving them certain phrases or words that they alone use. Andy Stanton's villainous Billy William III from the Mr Gum books always uses the word 'funty' instead of 'funny'. Lola from Lauren Child's Charlie and Lola books uses distinctive phrases like 'I will not ever never eat a tomato.' Beefy Bert in Horrid Henry only ever says, 'I dunno.' These aspects all add colour, brightening the characters as if you had turned up the contrast button on your TV.

Quirks

When a character originates with an *illustrator*, it will inevitably start visually: a boy in a wolfsuit, a patchwork elephant, a boy who loves stars. These characters are distinct from all others in a handful of important, well-defined ways that help to anchor them in readers' minds.

When a character originates with a *writer*, this visual aspect can get a little fuzzy. The character has to work much harder via the medium of the text and the alchemy of the reading brain in order to become visible. It also has to overcome the variables of thousands of different reading brains analysing and translating words into pictures. I have often been amazed by how the characters that I write – so visible to my own mind – can translate so differently in the minds of illustrators. I'm not sure the same is ever said of the reverse. Squishy McFluff, the invisible cat created by Pip Jones and illustrated by Ella Okstad, is an interesting example of a character that is visible in the pictures but invisible in the text.

A useful aspect of character development in illustrated books is to give your character at least one distinct visual feature. Tony Ross gave Horrid Henry a striped blue-and-yellow jumper; Jim Smith's Barry Loser got an enormous nose and curly hair. Hair is particularly good visual shorthand for character. Dennis the Menace's black explosion; Greg Heffley's three-pronged tuft; Tom Gates's sideways spikes: these character visuals are so strong that they can often be identified simply by their silhouettes.

Overall *style* of illustration can also tell a reader about a character. One reviewer of *Squishy McFluff Meets Mad Nana Dot* stated: 'The illustrations to this jaunty, rhyming narrative feature blocks of colour that sit just outside their prescribed borders, nicely reflecting the appealingly unruly heroine.' If your character is unruly, their picture should be, too. If neat, the opposite. Use strong lines for loud characters, gentle cross-hatching for quiet puppies. If you have loud characters and quiet puppies in the same story, use contrasting styles to emphasize the difference. Your characters will bounce off each other, more vivid than before.

Writers may not have the same tools at their disposal as illustrators, but they still need to give characters memorable quirks that lodge in the reader's mind, the way Paddington's duffel coat does. I have already talked about distinctive physical characteristics, but how about the way a character moves? Movement isn't something that can easily be conveyed by an illustration. It's a great opportunity for words to share some of the burden of characterization: a limp, a crablike scuttle, a constant blur of whirling limbs. Children learn to watch out for these cues and enjoy what they tell them about the characters.

Characters must change

The best stories are always stories about *change*. Characters should go through them like iron through a forge. To fulfil their potential, characters need to fail in order to win; they have to learn hard lessons; they must face unexpected situations that expand their understanding of themselves. They should end up a little different from how they were when everything began. This is the **character arc**.

Bilbo Baggins is one of the great characters of children's literature. At the start of *The Hobbit*, he lives a quiet, dull life in the Shire and is set on an unchanging path – until Gandalf the Grey strides into his life and throws a host of uninvited dwarves into his hobbit hole to clean out his larder and take him on a quest. Bilbo doesn't want to go. But over the course of the story, he discovers the adventurer inside himself. He is a different hobbit by the end of the book. It is *his* journey that grips the reader from start to finish. Without Bilbo's character arc, *The Hobbit* is just a story about dwarves and gold, elves and orcs and dragons. It has no heart.

Consistency

There is a difference, however, between a character that changes through the course of a story because of what happens to them, and a character who suddenly behaves differently for no reason at all. The changes within your character must be consistent, or the reader will lose their grip on the reality you are trying to conjure. Don't give a character a fear of water, then have them leaping into a swimming pool with a yell of delight *without explanation*. Plant reasons and clues along the way. Why has your character suddenly developed an ability to tightrope-walk when they are scared of heights? Why do they cuddle a cat in Chapter 2 when they are full of allergies in Chapter 1? Your character must change, yes, but they must change in a believable fashion – as part of their character arc. Change is rarely a lightning bolt that alters the horizon in a flash.

Workshop

Yes, we're back to fairy tales again for this workshop. Fairy tales rarely expand on characters, leaving a blank canvas for writers to develop. Take Snow White. Use your imagination – both sensory and inventive – to flesh her out: her looks, her personality. Develop her character arc from start to finish. Think of high and low points, and the order in which they occur. If you were thinking of her as a real person, fleshing her out and humanizing her, how do you think she might have changed by the end of the story? Do the same with Cinderella, and Jack from 'Jack and the Beanstalk'.

Next step

In the next chapter we are going to look at plotting, what it is and how to approach it. We will be breaking it down into three simple components, then fleshing it out further into what is known as the three-act structure. We will study the importance of maps, together with beginnings, middles and ends, and consider whether the best approach to a plot is via character or action.

8

Plotting

Philip Pullman, award-winning author of books such as *Northern Lights* and *The Firework Maker's Daughter*, once went on at length about writing things down on sticky notes, fixing them around the walls of his shed and arranging the scenes just so, before confessing to throwing the whole lot in the bin and plunging in. George Bernard Shaw also cheerfully claimed that, if he knew what would happen at the end of a story, he'd never start writing it.

It's a nice idea, this thought that you can produce a workable plot from nowhere. It sounds so effortless, flying along by the stretchy elastic of your underwear and hoping you'll end up somewhere sensible. It must be far more fun – more creative – than working out your story scene by scene, building plots and leaving nothing to chance.

But. BUT…

 Anne Rice

'The thing should have plot and character, beginning, middle and end. Arouse pity and then have a catharsis. Those were the best principles I was ever taught.'

Work at your plot

Shaw's method, or lack of one, is a risky approach when you are starting out. It's a little like my analogy of throwing yourself into the deep end of a swimming pool before you can swim; you make the mistake of assuming your great idea alone is enough to propel you safely through the water. It's not. Inexperience will drown you. What if you lose interest in your character, forget what your idea is about, write yourself into a corner? What if you realize, after weeks of work, that there is something so fundamentally flawed about your story that it's impossible to correct without stripping everything back to the beginning? All that work, wasted. Wouldn't it have been wiser to cover your bets and plan a little before you began?

So I'm going all in here, and stating outright: work at your plot before you begin to write. You should know where your story is going to end up before you start. You don't have to know every aspect of how you get there, but a rough idea is essential.

Starting a book is like visiting a strange town. You feel excited as you shake the dust of the road from your feet and stare at the exotic outskirts. You're going to have a great time in this place. You can feel it. You stride forward – and stop.

There are three roads branching off ahead of you. You want to get to the castle in the middle of the city, but you don't know which of the three roads to take because the signs are in a language you don't understand. You take a risk with the middle road because it seems like the most obvious route. Before you know it, the road swings off left, then right, then right again. You are winding through streets that are growing smaller and darker. You can't see the castle any more. You get an overwhelming sense of defeat and start longing for a nice cold drink back at your hotel. That feeling that you'd love this place has faded from your head. You wish you'd never come.

How different things would have been if you'd brought your guidebook. You could have pored over the little street maps at your leisure, and worked out the best way to the castle. You could have thought about the way the streets slotted together. You might even have felt so confident of finding your way that you would have allowed yourself to side-track every now and again – up some steps, through a tiny square you would never have guessed was there.

You would know that, at any time, you could return to the road and find the castle. You have it all under control.

How much detail you put into your plot is up to you, but I would say: don't produce a large-scale map. It will drain all of your creative energy and leave you little interest for the story writing itself. Sometimes you need a little freedom to take your story in an interesting direction – see my point about veering down side-streets while keeping the castle clearly in view.

Some people are born with a great sense of direction. Some aren't. For the purposes of this book, we'll assume you'd get lost in a supermarket. It does no harm to think the worst when starting out.

 ## Key idea

It's essential to know where you're going before you begin.

What is a plot?

A plot is what happens in your story. It is one step on from having an idea. The idea is the first line on the page; the plot fattens out that line and renders it in three dimensions. We have already looked into what makes a good idea. Now what makes a good plot?

E. M. Forster

'"The king died and then the queen died" is a story. "The king died, and then the queen died of grief," is a plot.'

First and foremost, a plot has to have *movement*. The very act of reading is one of movement: turning the pages, heading towards a conclusion. A badly plotted story lacks or misjudges that movement. Without movement, a story will sink into the mud, however wonderful the illustrations or poetic the language or strong the characters. Movement is created by asking the question: what happens next? If the reader is sufficiently interested in the answer, they will turn the page and your story will move in the right direction. But, like turning the key in the ignition of an elderly car, movement is in no way guaranteed. Just as you needed a spark for your idea, you now need a spark plug for your plot. You need combustion. You are setting a fire in order to make something happen.

Chuck Wendig

'A story that's just go go go breakneck speed is a horse that cannot sustain its gallop. You'll break the beast's back with that kind of pace. The downbeats, too, have a secret function: on a rollercoaster ride, the hills are the rush, but the valleys are where we learn to anticipate the next hill.'

This need for movement isn't just about maintaining a steady, forward motion. A plot also needs *pace*. No one wants to trundle along at an unchanging five miles an hour. A straight rocket ride is unsatisfactory, too. You need a mixture of fast and slow for your plot to work. Fast and slow don't just apply to the physical action; they apply to emotional action as well.

Chuck Wendig's comparison with a roller coaster is a great illustration of the art of pacing. You crank your way up a steep incline. You teeter for a moment, and then plunge down and round and round and up. You slow down just enough to catch your breath before it all starts again. You wind up to the biggest loop of all, and then slide home feeling marginally sick. I've a good mind to set you an exercise where you all have to go and ride a roller coaster to see what I mean – but for now, I will trust that your imaginations will see you right.

Plot also needs *conflict*. Characters chugging a smooth and unchanging course through life offer the reader nothing in the way of a plot. Conflict is the lifeblood of a good story, because it throws the characters off kilter and forces them to take action in interesting ways.

Think in threes

Movement, pace and conflict are the three elements that need to feature in a decent plot. Three is a magic number when you plot stories, particularly at this level. Three Little Pigs, Three Blind Mice,

Three Wise Men; three wishes, three chances, three dreams. Two is too quick and flat. Four is unnecessarily complicated. Three, as Goldilocks discovers, is just right, because it allows for a beginning, a middle and an end. When viewed in the shape of a triangle, the number three graphically illustrates the movement you need when plotting stories: low, high, then back to low again.

At its most basic level, a plot is comprised of – you've guessed it – three elements. One: setting the scene. Two: presenting the problem. Three: resolving the problem. The first and second elements must propel a reader towards the final, resolving element, providing the necessary movement. This is what's known as the **story arc.** While not strictly a triangle, the story arc rises and falls in the same way.

- **Setting the scene** What is the story about? Aesop's best-known fable, 'The Hare and the Tortoise', is about a hare and a tortoise having a race. The prospect of such an ill-matched contest immediately throws up questions that move the plot on.
- **Presenting the problem** What is the problem? It is, of course, is that the odds are heavily stacked in favour of the Hare. The Tortoise is clearly in over his head. There is no possible way he can win the race. Or… is there?
- **Resolving the problem** What happens? Thanks to the Hare's overbearing confidence and mid-race snooze, the slow but steady Tortoise wins the race.

Movement, pace and conflict are all present in this basic outline. So far, so good.

There are two further elements to consider within this most simple of plot frameworks.

First: as Aesop does in 'The Hare and the Tortoise', *resolve your problem in an unexpected way.* No one wants to read about the Hare winning the race. By having the Tortoise win, you throw a spanner in the works of the normal progression of things. You subvert the obvious. However, no one wants to read a wholly unlikely story either, so any unexpected resolution must be believable. It can't be a case of, oh, the Tortoise wins because the Hare mysteriously turns into a sunflower. You must also avoid happy coincidence, where the Hare happens to sprain his foot in the last 50 metres – yay for unexpected tussocks. The Tortoise won because he was steady where the Hare was foolish.

Which brings me neatly to the second element: *characters must play an active part in the resolution of your plot.* They must be masters of their own destinies.

In *Clown*, the little toy clown of the title sits in a dustbin at the start of the story. Quentin Blake originally wanted to draw a cat pulling the clown out. He decided instead to give the clown full responsibility for his own escape. Illustrations show the little clown wriggling and squirming his own way to freedom, allowing the reader to see and appreciate the character's efforts. The result is that the reader feels more invested in both the character and the plot.

Your own unexpected resolution must also come down to something one of your characters does. The Hare loses the race because he's over-confident. The Tortoise wins because he sticks to the plan. We believe the story because we see for ourselves the Tortoise's steady character, and we notice the way that the Hare brings about his own downfall. No lightning bolts, no dreams, no fortunate accidents or helpful strangers popping up from behind hedges. No *deus ex machina*, either. This expression – meaning 'god out of the machine' – originated with the Greeks, who would lower or raise on to a stage a cage containing an actor in the role of a God, who would sort things out with a thunderbolt and/or a speech. Modern audiences don't buy it. Avoid it.

Don't, by the way, assume that a planned and logical approach means a dull resolution. Simple, logical progression can and must still result in unexpected endings.

Snapshot

Think about the story 'The North Wind and the Sun' that we talked about in Chapter 1: Starting out. Break this story down into the three basic elements of its plot:

- What is it about?
- What is the problem?
- What happens?

Then ask yourself:

Is the ending unexpected? Is the ending realistic?

Are the characters active in resolving the problem?

The 'elevator pitch'

 Uncredited editor,
www.parents.com

*'If you can't tell me what your book is about in one short
paragraph, then you don't know what it's about and I'm not
interested.'*

Picture the scene. You are riding in an elevator and someone is
making chitchat with you. That person happens to be a publishing
professional, so you tell them you are writing a book. If you're
lucky, they will ask you what it's about. You ideally need to be able
to tell them in 30 seconds or less, before the doors go *bing* and
you lose your audience. Spending time at the planning stage on
reducing your plot into its essence with the three-questions approach
described in the Snapshot above could spell your big break.

I once called an editor in a fit of bravado with an idea for a story.
When she asked me what it was about, I froze, and waffled, and
proved both to her and myself that it wasn't going to work as a
book. When writing for children, you should be able to reduce your
story into situation/problem/resolution. Put simply: if you can't
reduce your idea, it's not going to work.

'So, this "The Hare and the Tortoise" story, Aesop. What's it
about?'

'It's about a hare and a tortoise having a race where the hare thinks
he's got it in the bag, but against all the odds the tortoise wins.'

Blurb

Blurb is that brief, punchy paragraph that you see on the back cover
of a book. It is different from an elevator pitch, but just as useful
when it comes to focusing your mind on your plot.

Good blurb isn't designed to reveal too much. Its main purpose
is to hook the reader and make them open the book to find out
for themselves what happens. Writing the blurb for your story is

excellent practice for reducing your ideas to their essence in an exciting, attention-grabbing way while still keeping certain elements to yourself. Pamela Cleaver in her book *Writing for Children* summarizes blurb thus:

> WHEN *something happens (your inciting incident) / *protagonist (name) PURSUES *a goal (what the protagonist wants). BUT WILL HE SUCCEED WHEN *name of antagonist / puts obstacles in the way (list some exciting incidents)?

So the blurb for 'The Hare and the Tortoise' might look something like this:

> When the Hare challenges the Tortoise to a race, the tortoise is confident that he can win. But will he succeed when the Hare is the fastest animal in the wood?

If you're struggling with your plot, writing a piece of blurb can help you discover what might be needed to round your story off with a bang. If you've worked out your plot already, writing blurb can still help to crystallize your ideas. Win–win.

Write

Look again at your three-sentence summary of 'The North Wind and the Sun'. Can you run your three answers together into one single, punchy elevator pitch? Practise saying the sentence out loud. Can you improve it?

Write the blurb for the same story, and compare the differences.

Of course, Aesop's fables are famously simple stories, often running to just two or three paragraphs with the moral given in the final sentence. The linear progression of their plotting suits the direct approach of a picture book and the demands of a very young audience. But when you have up to 10,000 words plus pictures to consider for a piece of young fiction, can you plot your story in the same way?

Take a look at the longer, slightly more complex story 'Rumpelstiltskin'. What is it about? A young girl who has to spin straw into gold. What is the problem? If she doesn't succeed in her impossible task, she'll die. What happens? She succeeds with the help of an imp.

That may be a true reflection of the first part of the plot, but it's not the whole story, is it? What about the ever-expanding piles of straw and the girl's desperate promises to the imp that she'll hand over her firstborn child? What about afterwards, when the girl becomes a queen and the imp returns to claim the child? What about the three chances (that magic number again!) to guess the imp's name that are the Queen's only hope, the last-minute relief of learning the imp's name in the nick of time, and the final satisfying resolution? The longer the story, the more room you have to make your way from the beginning to the end. You can fit in a few more problems. You might even add a subplot, perhaps develop the girl's relationship with the father who makes that fatal boast about his daughter's gold-spinning abilities in the first place. Cast your mind back to the beginning of this chapter, when I made the point about having a map so that you allow time to meander while never losing sight of the castle. This is where that map starts coming in very handy.

But if three questions are no longer enough, what is the alternative?

The three-act structure

Plot is what happens. Structure is how you make it happen.

In the three-act structure:

- **Act One** provides what is known as 'the inciting incident' (what starts the story) and ends with a cliffhanger.
- **Act Two** takes you to a solid midpoint, and ends where all appears to be lost.
- **Act Three** resolves everything, preferably with a twist.

We're still dealing in threes, but we are breaking down those threes into smaller components. The original three-question approach is still lurking inside this new framework if you look closely. So is that unexpected (yet realistic) ending. But things are a bit stretchier. You have more room to breathe and move around. Understanding the three-act structure, and developing the confidence to play around within its confines, is a crucial tool in your writing kit.

A Pixar executive once used the analogy of a poker game when talking about the three-act structure:

1 You are dealt a hand of cards (the inciting incident).

2 You decide to bet (the end of Act One).

3 You go all in at the point of no return (the midpoint).

4 You appear to lose (the end of Act Two).

5 You manage to win against the odds (the final twist).

I would beg a stage 6 – you do a celebratory dance – because everyone loves to revel in a happy ending, particularly when writing for children. I always enjoyed the end of one of Enid Blyton's Faraway Tree stories because the entire last chapter was devoted to the Land of Parties without a hint of jeopardy. After all the shenanigans with Dame Slap ('Snap' in modern editions) and the Abominable Snowman, both the characters and the readers deserved jellies and party games. Grown-ups think this way, too. I challenge you to watch the party at the end of *The Return of the Jedi* and not smile.

If we apply the three-act structure to the story of Rumpelstiltskin, we can see how it works:

Case study: *Rumpelstiltskin* and the three-act structure

The inciting incident (you are dealt a hand of cards): The girl finds herself locked in a room after her father the miller makes his terrible boast to the King – that his beautiful daughter can spin straw into gold. Right away, the heroine is in a dilemma, which makes you want to read on.

The end of Act One (you decide to bet): By thinking of this story as a play, I think it's easy to locate the best place for the end of Act One: the girl asks the imp for his help when he appears in her locked tower room. You know promising things to the imp can only spell trouble, and that the girl's action – putting herself in the imp's power – will set this in motion. This is a point where you want to leave your main character in a tricky situation, which will ensure you return after the interval, melting ice cream in hand, to find out what happens next. Thinking of this as the 'you decide to bet' stage should also remind you to make sure your characters are driving the action and aren't just passive chess pieces.

The midpoint (you go all in): The midpoint is always a tough one. It needs to be the place where the story is in full flow and you don't want to put it down for a moment. I would put the midpoint at the place where the imp returns to claim the new Queen's firstborn child as promised. The stakes couldn't be higher. As with the end of Act One, the main character's action – promising her child to the imp in the first place – directly influences the plot, bringing us back to my earlier point about making sure the characters are masters of their own destinies.

The end of Act Two (you appear to lose): The Queen has three days to guess the imp's name in order to save her child. On the first two days her attempts have all been wrong. The imp's great prize is within a fingernail's reach. If her guesses on the third day are wrong, she'll lose her child for ever! HOW WILL SHE GET OUT OF THIS ONE? is always a good question to ask at this stage. Throw as much trouble at your main character as you possibly can, then throw a bit more. How can you possibly leave the theatre to catch the last bus now?

The final twist (you manage to win against the odds): Everything is stacked against the Queen ever discovering the imp's name. At the last moment, one of her servants returns to the palace with news of a strange creature found dancing around and singing his name for all to hear. When the imp appears at the court for the third and final time, convinced that he will get the child, the Queen toys with him twice before revealing the right name on her third attempt (three strikes again). Phew. By stacking the odds as high as you can, you make the resolution all the more satisfying.

Celebratory dance: It's more of an enraged stomp really as Rumpelstiltskin smashes a hole through the floorboard with his foot, but no less satisfying for all that.

While this breakdown works perfectly well, I do have an issue with this version. In the ideal story structure, as stated several times above, the main character needs to be the master of her own destiny. Putting the Queen in a ninja outfit and camouflage paint and sending her out into the dark depths of the wood to spy on Rumpelstiltskin for herself instead of giving the job to a nameless servant would, in my opinion, both improve the story and put more flesh on the character's bones. What do you think?

So that's how other people do it. What about you?

Let's take a look at working up a plot for Ernie the line-dancing earthworm. Remember him from the opening chapter? I told you we'd revisit him. We'll take the three-question approach to begin with:

1 What is it about? An earthworm who wants to line-dance.

2 What is the problem? He doesn't have any legs.

The first two elements are in place. But what about the third and final element?

3 How can Ernie overcome his problem?

This is the part where all the 'teach yourself' manuals in the world won't help. You just have to have faith in your own imagination – that muscle you have been diligently exercising since the start of this book, both visually and inventively – and jump in. Blurt out thoughts, write them down, sketch them out. Don't be afraid of weird tangents, don't panic about plotting yourself into a corner. It's early days in the life of your story. And, unlike in the real world, you can write your way out of *anything*. You are an elemental force of nature. Your plot is utterly subject to your will. Know this and enjoy the feeling of power.

Cressida Cowell, author-illustrator of the How to Train Your Dragon middle-grade fiction series, takes perverse delight in regularly ruining her hero's life. In the final book of the series, *How to Fight a Dragon's Fury*, she abandons Hiccup the unconscious hero on a beach infested with sand-sharks, with two black eyes and an arm purple and swollen from the venomous bite of a vampire spydragon. His clothes are in tatters, there are dragon scratches all over him. He has no boat, no weapons and no friends to help him, apart from a tiny, elderly dragon who has just been hit by a poisoned dart. And, to round off his problems, he's lost his memory as well. And yet she gets him out of the whole disaster intact. *Anything* is possible when you are the one wielding the pen.

For the purposes of this exercise, let's say Ernie teams up with another line-dance-loving earthworm friend, thereby providing two 'legs', with each 'leg' taking responsibility for half of the routine. The problem is not only resolved but it is resolved in an unexpected, character-driven way. Tada! You have created a plot.

Snapshot

Develop the three-question plotline of Ernie the line-dancing earthworm into the three-act structure. You can find an alternative ending, or use the one that I have suggested. Keep Ernie at the centre of the action.

Beginning, middle and end

Jean-Luc Godard

'A story should have a beginning, a middle and an end, but not necessarily in that order.'

Jean-Luc Godard's quote is fun, but dangerous when writing and illustrating for young children. Children are still making sense of the world in a clear and linear way: want whole ice-cream tub, eat whole ice-cream tub, feel sick. If you start messing around with the holy triumvirate of beginning/middle/end for this age group, you can cause confusion.

Luckily for you, the strange towns that comprise picture books and illustrated children's fiction are small places. There are only a couple of little roads that could lead you to the main point of interest: the castle, or the windmill, or the local Museum of Dried Fruit. But, to make the most of your trip, you still need to work out a good route, and a good route – like a good story – needs a beginning, a middle and an end.

Snapshot

Find a map of a town that you don't know. Work out a route from the car park to the town's main place of interest. Think about the benefits of going straight to the place you are aiming for, or reach it via a meandering route. When do you think you would need a rest, and when would you need extra encouragement to reach your destination? Are there steps, hills, boring bits that might need energizing in some way? Work out an itinerary as if you were touring the town. Hold this idea of a map in your mind when you plot your story.

THE BEGINNING

Let's start at the car park I asked you to visualize a few chapters ago. It's where most visits to strange towns begin, after all. We're in the car park and – what?

This is where many first-time writers and illustrators make their first mistake. They talk about the car park at great length. They draw the parking meters in minute detail. If you think about plotting a story in this way, you can see at once what a bad idea it is to start somewhere so very, very dull. Factor in the attention span of your audience – you have a matter of seconds, sometimes even less with very small children – and you will swiftly find yourself alone, the only sound that of gently falling rain on car roofs, the only sight a ball of tumbleweed rolling past the recycling bins.

Something needs to happen, fast. You need to engage your reader with a great character, and you need to get your plot moving. And both of these things need to happen on the opening page. In the case of a picture book, you may have only 20 or 30 words to grab your readers' interest, or one or two pictures. You'll lose them if you stay in that car park one second longer than necessary. So how do you do it?

The idea for *Elmer*, a picture book about difference and acceptance, came to author-illustrator David McKee after his daughter was racially abused in the street. The 1968 book begins as follows:

There was once a herd of elephants. Elephants young, elephants old, elephants tall or fat or thin. Elephants like this, that or the other, all different but all happy and all the same colour. All, that is, except Elmer.

In 39 words, McKee sets up Elmer's world and introduces Elmer, albeit in a reverse-psychology kind of way (Elmer isn't in the first picture). Not only that, but he also gives himself a great visual opportunity to draw 20 grey elephants, all ever so slightly different from one other. The words and pictures, together with the tempting absence of Elmer himself, makes us ask that crucial question – provides that essential movement – which will lead us to turn the page. What makes Elmer different?

How might you begin a story about Ernie the earthworm that will catch your reader's interest in both the character and the plot, right from the start?

Ernie is an earthworm.

Your character has no immediate aspect of interest. Your opening line asks no questions, it presents no difficulties. It kick-starts nothing resembling a plot. As it presently stands, my world won't end if I don't turn over the page to find out what happens next.

Ernie is an earthworm who loves line-dancing.

This still doesn't work. You've given me nothing about Ernie's character other than his species, as before. The rest of the sentence is static and self-contained. If Ernie loves line-dancing, it is plain that he has already worked out a way around that small leg-related issue. His wormy little life is sorted. Again: no reason to turn over the page. Fine for the planning stage; not fine for your opening line, your all-important hook.

Ernie is an earthworm with a problem.

Now we're getting somewhere. Can you feel the question twitching at the back of your mind? By starting with a problem, you are away.

Key idea

The opening line for your plot and the opening line for your text serve different functions. A plotting sentence sets the scene, but an opening line has to grab you.

Of course, this is just looking at the plot from the perspective of the text. If you *draw* Ernie with enough character, even with that flat opening sentence you may yet turn over the engine in your reader's mind and get going. John Burningham opens his classic picture book *Mr Gumpy's Outing* with four simple words: 'This is Mr Gumpy.' It is hardly the sentence of the century, but when it's matched with the illustration, the reader is drawn onwards to learn more about this cheery-looking man with his squashed brown hat. But given that you are just starting out, I wouldn't advise giving the pictures all the work, any more than I would advise the same of the words. Aim for the best of both.

Focus point

Illustrated books use words and pictures to tell the story. They should share the load, not mirror each other.

Snapshot

Here are four openings to well-known picture books. What questions do they pose? Why does the reader want to turn the page?

Rosie the hen went for a walk.

(Pat Hutchins, *Rosie's Walk*)

This is Olivia. She is good at lots of things.

(Ian Falconer, *Olivia*)

Down down down the dark street they came, quiet as mice, stealthy as shadows.

(Peter Harris and Deborah Allwright, *The Night Pirates*)

There once was a boy and the boy loved stars very much.

(Oliver Jeffers, *How to Catch a Star*)

Try to find these books in your library or local bookshop so you can study the pictures in combination with the text. Do the pictures raise other ideas or pose different questions?

Some picture books spin out the start more than Elmer, but you are still drawn onwards by the force of the storytelling. Maurice Sendak's *Where the Wild Things Are* takes six pages of text and pictures before you could say that the story has begun. Shirley Hughes takes even longer with *Dogger*, setting up Dave's relationship with his soft toy and his family for eight pages before Dogger is lost on page 9. Some books leave the first picture alone to hook you and draw you into the story: Chris Haughton's *A Bit Lost* wordlessly shows a little owl falling out of a tree. With such variety out there, how do you know the best way to start *your* book?

You don't. But I urge you not to run before you can walk. The best advice I can give you as a first-timer is to *get out of the car park*. And remember that you have an advantage. You are writing an illustrated book. The pictures will move the story along as well as the words.

Snapshot

Study the following sentence:

> There is a fat, friendly tiger at the bottom of the sea, standing on a bed of coral with fish swimming into its mouth, apparently thinking that it's a cave.

It describes the opening page of Victoria Turnbull's picture book *The Sea Tiger*. Victoria won the Association of Illustrators' New Talent Award in 2013 for her story about a merboy's imaginary friend. She wrote the book as part of her MA in Children's Book Illustration, and won the award before the book was published. It was shortlisted for the Kate Greenaway Medal in 2015. Victoria uses only five words on this opening page, with the rest relayed visually. What do you think the words might be? You'll find the answer at the end of this chapter. (There's a clue earlier in this chapter, too.)

THE MIDDLE

You're getting hot and bored. The castle doesn't feel like it's getting any closer, and the car park's miles away. You're running out of snacks, and it's that annoying time of day when the shops close for two hours in the hot midday sun. You've sat down on a bench and can feel a yawn coming on. How can you maintain your own interest, let alone the interest of your readers?

Firstly: *get off the bench.* Movement and pacing are never so important as when you're in the middle of your story. The middle is all about ratcheting up the tension. It's that part of the roller coaster when you rise and fall, rise a bit more and fall a bit further, rise even higher... and so on. The middle is where Ernie's choices become tougher, where he has an accelerating mass of problems – three is good, if you remember – that he needs to overcome. The middle is where the monster eats Bernard in David McKee's *Not Now, Bernard.* In *Jamela's Dress* by Niki Daly, the middle is where Jamela realizes the consequences of dancing through the streets dressed up in her mother's finest dress fabric (in short: trouble). The middle of Quentin Blake's *Clown* sees the little clown sailing towards a window in an apartment block in one large single-page illustration, at which point his luck finally changes for the better.

The middle is the pivot on which the seesaw depends. Which way will it tip? If you cast your mind back to the chapter on series fiction where I outlined a chapter breakdown for my book *Space Penguins: Star Attack!* , the middle part has penguin astronauts winning and losing at battles that become increasingly important, creating a 'wavy' effect on the narrative plotting graph. Keep the reader guessing, keep the action coming. Ramp up the emotion. Do something drastic. The middle has to be the most exciting part, not the part where everything drags. It has to be the part where a tiger charges at you from an unexpected side street.

Case study: *Dogger* by Shirley Hughes

Let's take a look at an example of a middle section, in Shirley Hughes's *Dogger*. The inciting incident – when Dave is dealt his hand of cards – is when Dave loses his precious soft toy Dogger at the beginning of the story. Dave's misery is compounded at the school fair by his sister Bella, who keeps winning things: first a three-legged race, then a huge teddy in the raffle. He's as low as he can be: the first dip in the roller coaster.

Then, suddenly, Dave sees Dogger sitting on the bric-a-brac stall with a five-pence price tag round his neck. Dogger isn't lost any more! We've been down – now we're on top of the world. But as anyone who has ridden a roller coaster will tell you, there's more than one dip in the middle of the ride. Dave can't find his parents to ask them for five pence to buy Dogger back. He finally finds Bella, and drags her to the bric-a-brac stall ... to find that a little girl has bought Dogger and refuses to sell him back.

This is the second roller-coaster dip. It feels even worse than the first, partly because of the joy and relief that precedes it. Contrast is one of your greatest weapons in the middle part of a story. The reader powers on, breathless to know: how will he get out of this one? (I told you this question was useful.) This corresponds to Stage 4 of the three-act structure – the end of Act 2, where you appear to lose. The roller coaster is at its peak, ready for the final twist.

Snapshot

Think of three problems Ernie the line-dancing earthworm has to face before his problem can be resolved. Try to make each problem bigger than the last.

THE END

Henry Wadsworth Longfellow

'Great is the art of beginning, but greater is the art of ending.'

However much detail you choose to go into when you plot your story, focus as much as you can on *how it will all end*. The ending is THE most important part of your planning. If you fail to deliver, you are letting down the reader who has bothered to invest their time and energy into your story. You have to produce something that will bring a reader back time and again to relive the delights of your creation. That is the mark of a really good story.

So how do you deliver that knock-out punch?

I once visited the castle town of Obidos, in Portugal. We approached the town from the railway station, up a steep slope towards a scruffy gateway in a bit of wall. We had more than a few misgivings that this place wasn't going to be nearly as great as the pictures in the guidebook had suggested. We were in that roller-coaster dip, that middle part of our journey.

It was only when we reached the top of the hill and stood in the scruffy gateway – not quite as scruffy up close as it had appeared from a distance – that we appreciated just how perfect our approach had been. We had inadvertently come into the *top* of the town. The castle, streets and houses stretched down the hill ahead of us within a complete ring of medieval walls, giving us a perfect yet completely unexpected view of the whole.

It would have been different if we had approached the town from the other direction. We would have known what we were in for, because it would all have been laid out ahead of us to observe as we approached. We might even have stopped at a café outside the gates, deciding that we'd seen all we needed to see. The contrast between our genuine midway misgivings and the rush of delight we felt at the unexpected conclusion to our journey is what you should aim for in your plotting. Give your readers the ending they have earned, but give it to them in an unexpected way. Provide them with that final twist, Stage 5 in your three-act structure. A celebratory dance is sure to follow. With luck, a rereading, too.

When you cross your finishing line, it has to be with a neat resolution that both satisfies *and* surprises. Make sure that you've answered all the questions you raised at the beginning. There is no excuse for leaving loose ends flapping in the wind. Equally, don't throw in any surprises at this stage without having laid a trail well in advance. Don't ascribe the whole journey to a dream in the style of Bobby Ewing circa 1986. This is where plotting is so vital. If you've done it right, you will have given yourself ample opportunity to seed your surprises in suitably sneaky ways. Illustrators can have a lot of fun with this, drawing details that only become important at the end of the story. In *Dogger*, Dave's big sister Bella persuades the little girl to swap Dogger for the teddy she has won in the raffle. Readers have glimpsed the teddy several times – on the raffle table, under Bella's arm – before it plays its vital role in bringing the story to a happy ending. The idea is seeded. Bella's gesture is a surprise, yet not a surprise. *If You Go Walking in Tiger Wood* by Alan Durant and Debbie Boon has two children skipping through the jungle watching out for tigers, when all the time the tigers are watching out for them. The readers know this, but the children in the story don't. The different layers deepen the experience of the whole. Those layers don't appear at the last minute. They have been *planned*.

You must also double-check your character arc. Has your main character had real ups and downs, successes and failures throughout the plot? Have the efforts of the journey transformed them, but still left them as the character your reader first invested in? Shunned to begin with, the odd creatures of Kathryn Cave and Chris Riddell's *Something Else* take their experiences and turn them to the good when they welcome the third, much odder 'something else' to join their gang in the final page-turn. The ending is surprising, satisfying and logical all in one go.

Case study: The cover illustration

This is a good moment to think about the book cover because a good one has aspects of beginning, middle *and* end. It is the beginning of the reading experience for most children. It is likely to feature one of those roller-coaster moments in the middle of your story – the climax, the point of no return, the heart-thumping appearance of the Gruffalo. And although it will always be the first thing a young reader sees, the right cover illustration is only likely to suggest itself at the end of the whole process, after the story is complete.

In many ways, it can be the most difficult part of the book: it needs to suggest what the story is about but not give too much away. The opening line or page must hook the reader, but the cover must prime them for that hook. If you are the writer, the cover isn't something you need to trouble yourself with because it's the editors and designers who will decide which scene in your story might best draw in a reader, and they will commission an illustration accordingly. If you are the illustrator, the cover will be of more interest. You may find that the image you create for that heart-stopping midway point is perfect for the cover; you may find that the editors and designers want a new piece of artwork altogether. Gather ideas, but don't commit yourself until everyone is in agreement. You'll save yourself a lot of effort.

Action-based plots versus character-based plots

I have said above that all good children's plots need strong, relatable characters. The only way you can get away with thinner characters is if your plot has the action coming so thick and fast that your characters are somehow secondary. The heart-thumping nature of stories like these – kids running away from baddies and exploding volcanoes, tightrope-walking over Niagara Falls – can sometimes be enough on its own. You will, for example, often find that plot overrides characters in reading-scheme books, where the aim is to get a child turning the pages. However, reading schemes aside, you will almost always find that purely action-based stories are best left to a more visual medium like film or TV. The slower, deeper experience that you get from a book needs well-rounded characters to keep you reading, where a film needs only helicopter crashes and speedboat chases to keep you watching. People are often disappointed by the films of their favourite books because the speed of the medium has to strip away all nuances of character in favour of action. Likewise, films and TV shows rarely translate well to books because the characters aren't strong enough to carry the story across the rugged, slow-moving terrain of a page.

If you can find the sweet spot between action and character that appeals both on the page and on the screen, good luck to you. You're on to a winner.

Workshop

By now I hope that you have come up with an idea for your story – more than likely you already had several before you began reading this book. So for this workshop I would like you to start planning the plot. Try to use at least two of the structural techniques we have looked at in this chapter. And, as you plot and plan, try to keep that all-important ending – the hilltop castle – in your sights.

Next step

In the next chapter we will look at how to set the scene with foreground and background, using all the senses, doing your research, knowing what to include and what to leave out. We will consider how to move from place to place without interrupting the flow of a story; how places can be used as catalysts; time, weather and mood; and the role of the illustrator in this particular part of the process. We will also look at keeping your settings consistent, and introduce the idea of a 'bible' to use as reference when world-building at a more complex level.

Answer to Snapshot

I am the Sea Tiger.

9

Setting the scene

You have characters. You have a plot. Now you need a setting: a textured, believable world where the action can take place.

In illustrated books, the setting features in two ways. The first is the written context in which you place your characters as they follow that swooping, tightly plotted narrative arc that you have developed. The second is the visual context as imagined by the illustrator to accompany the action.

Setting is where an illustrator can come into their own. Places have a reassuring solidity to them. Your illustrator is the one who will make your imagined world real, with all the details you can't include in your writing. Your vision and theirs won't necessarily match. And that is the beauty of illustrated books. You might write a book that you have always imagined as taking place in your hometown. The illustrator imagines it taking place in *her* hometown – or in an Amazonian rainforest, or an underwater city. You end up with a multi-faceted story you could never have imagined by yourself.

World-building

> Down at the bottom of the garden, there is a pile of flowerpots behind an old watering can and a patch of nettles. A dandelion clock grows in the middle, and bluebells grow around the edges. The flowerpots aren't much to look at. This is probably why you never noticed them before.

The quote above is taken from one of my books, *Imps Are Wimps*, one of the Naughty Fairies series, which sits in the 'series fiction' category of young fiction for five- to eight-year-olds. It was an in-house idea: a concept dreamed up by editors who went out and found a writer – in this case, me – to build the world they had imagined. For Naughty Fairies, the brief was simply 'St Trinian's with wings', leaving me lots of flexibility to come up with characters, plots and settings.

The setting for Naughty Fairies came before the characters (who, in turn, came before the plots). I knew that fairies were small, and I had grown up in the firm belief that fairies lived at the bottom of the garden. So I started each book with the phrase, 'Down at the bottom of the garden' and visualized a world in miniature.

From there, I started work on the *foreground*. I built up a picture of the Naughty Fairies' immediate world: the scruffy flowerpots and jam jars of their school, St Juniper's. I gave them a dandelion clock to keep the time, and bluebells to ring between lessons. I added a cobweb trampoline for fun, and made sure to include it in several of the stories so that it earned its place. Although this was a world that would be peopled by fairies, I made sure to include plenty of familiar elements for readers to identify with: lessons, classrooms, pets, food.

Key idea

When world-building, keep elements of your setting familiar so that your readers have something with which to anchor themselves in their new and strange surroundings.

Once I had established my foreground, I thought about the *background*, which I wanted to use to give a sense of scale: the House where the Humans lived; the Pond, which I wanted to feature in one of the books; the Hedge, where I had a feeling I could place one or two of the adventures; the Field with its hollow Wood Stump for fairy parties and meetings, and, most importantly, Ambrosia Academy, the rival fairy school, where the fairies were all pink and pretty and well behaved, and entirely designed to contrast and conflict with my Naughty Fairies and help to bring them to life.

When I had figured out what went where, I drew a map. A real map this time, not an imaginary plot map of castles and car parks. Much of it was based on my own garden, with artistic licence employed for the Field beyond. Because I had spent time building it up in my mind, I knew exactly where the fairy dormitories were, whether to turn left or right when the fairies left their classrooms, and how many floors were in the Butterfly Stables. I could now place my characters convincingly among the weeds and jam jars as they went about their mischief. I had a three-dimensional world. I had a setting.

Key idea

Think about your setting in layers: a detailed foreground where the main action will take place and sketchier but no less solid background to anchor that foreground.

With a series as place-specific as Naughty Fairies, there was real value in spending time in the early stages planning the setting to this degree. If you are telling a story about a little girl living in a normal town and going to a normal school, you probably don't need this level of detail to make your setting convincing. Everyone knows about high streets and bus shelters, and roads and rivers and bridges. Everyone already has some kind of reference point in place. You talk about a bridge: your reader will picture a bridge. It may not be exactly the same bridge as you were visualizing as you wrote the story, but how much does it matter? If the specifics of your bridge directly affect your plot, it matters and you should spend time developing it so that your readers are right alongside you in the mechanics of your story. If your bridge could be any kind of bridge and the plot would still function regardless, you shouldn't.

The setting for your story should be *solid*.

Solidity doesn't mean pages of intricate detail on the shape of the pavements and the colour of the bricks. Solidity means taking the firmest hold on people's imaginations and creating dependable, three-dimensional images in their heads. We don't need many words to be able to create that solidity if there are pictures to support it. We just need those words to be memorable; to draw on our senses and create a firm, unwavering image upon which we can project the action.

In some cases, your setting almost becomes a character in its own right, as in Terry Pratchett's Discworld or Mervyn Peake's Gormenghast. If you can achieve this level of personality in your world, well and good. Use it.

Making a 'bible'

If you are planning on doing some serious world-building – creating a setting with lots of intricate and important details – it's worthwhile putting all the information into a 'bible'. This could be in a Word document, in a notebook, on a pinboard detailing how characters dress and which building is where and whether Muggles are allowed into Hogwarts and so on. This will help you to stay consistent. If you get a publishing deal further down the line, this 'bible' will become invaluable for editors and illustrators, too.

When compiling your 'bible', you should include place names, topography (is your setting in the mountains or by the seaside?), whether it's a happy/quiet/busy/dangerous place, whether the people are small or magical or have any defining features. Engage your senses. Is there an overriding colour or visual impression that you want to convey? Does the town have a special smell, are there particular animal noises on the farm? Fit in as many details as you can. Close your eyes and move around its streets, hills and fields. Get to know it so well that you could write pages about its architecture and population.

Fill your 'bible' with physical items as well. You could include postcards, magazine articles, pieces of fabric that suggest your main character's perfect outfit, photographs you have taken that seem to capture the mood of the world you are trying to create.

Now comes the difficult part. Use your bible to inform your story, but don't feel you have to splurge it all out. Most especially, don't splurge it all out in one go. It's tempting to think, 'I've researched newt spawning grounds to the *n*th degree, I deserve to showcase every aspect of my efforts.' But your book isn't about you. It's about your readers. You have to be selfless and sacrifice yourself on the altar of Wikipedia so your readers don't have to. Trust me when I say your level of expertise will show as you pick and choose just those aspects of pond life that will enhance and/or drive your plot. Your readers need only to feel that they are in safe hands as you tell your story. Just give them the impression that you know exactly where you are, and where you are taking them. *Impression*, not chapter and verse.

Your in-depth knowledge must never obscure the reason you're telling the story: your characters and their journey through your plot. J. K, Rowling knows Diagon Alley well enough to convince us of its existence in *Harry Potter and the Philosopher's Stone*, but she keeps our attention on the characters throughout. Because Harry is going into the shops, running his fingers through tubs of beetle eyes, hearing the soft hoots of the owls and experiencing Ollivander's wand shop for himself, we are right there with him. If Diagon Alley had been described without Harry interacting with the shopkeepers and their goods, it would have been an imaginative description of a magical street but nothing else. It would have lacked the extra dimension that pulls a reader inside.

Consistency

Be *consistent* with your setting. An uneven bake never impresses.

Check the physical aspects first. A front door can't change from blue to red without explanation. If the town hall is on the left of the square in Chapter 1, then mysteriously moves to the right side in Chapter 2, your reader will lose that magical sense of being inside the book and will instead feel confused and disengaged. Don't think as you lurch from one half-considered room to the next, 'That's fine, no one will notice that I don't know how the rooms I'm writing about fit together.' Children, in particular, can be very beady about details like this. Don't disappoint them.

Don't disappoint the agents and editors you hope will be reading your story either. If they notice anything sloppy about your setting, they will reject your manuscript right away. No story is so good that consistency fails to matter.

Be consistent with other aspects of your setting, too. What kind of feeling does the place have? How does it smell? Is it a good place to be, or a bad one? Does it constantly rain? Are all the houses built of stone, or brick, or diamonds? Sitting on the fence makes for a dull environment that's hard to grasp. Remember what I said about *bold lines*. If you find any aspect of your world fuzzy, then your reader will find it fuzzy, too. Put in the time to familiarize yourself with the terrain before you start writing. Your story will then have that ring of authenticity it needs if it is going to transport the reader to your world.

Setting and genre

The relative importance of setting changes according to genre. Obviously, a book with an historical aspect will need more attention, setting-wise, than a book with a contemporary one. That said, never overdo things: children – and adults for that matter – don't turn to fiction for a history lesson. In any story there should be only *just* enough setting for the characters to be vivid and comprehensible and the plot to seem natural and logical (at least in terms if the world you have built). Such detail should be integrated almost invisibly into the story, not laid on top with a shovel, in plain sight.

HISTORICAL SETTINGS

These are tough. Not only do you have to think about the basic logistics of moving your characters from A to B, you have to think about the sort of practicalities than never afflict modern characters. How does your character move from town to town? How do they communicate over long distances? What kind of shops did they have in Victorian times? Were people riding bicycles in 1842? (Answer: not really, and certainly not riding bicycles as we know them today.) You are also giving your illustrator reference headaches. What kind of skirts did ladies wear in 1930? What shoes, what hairstyles? A few details are fun, but like everything in children's books, they must earn their keep, affecting the action. Is your story dependent on a horse-drawn carriage? An open-top omnibus?

If you are writing a picture book, avoid any setting that requires too much historical exposition (background information) – partly because your audience is too young to appreciate the details, partly because you only have a maximum of 1,000 words in which to explain the background *and* tell the story. A few historical details can be nice: long swishy dresses, big hats, gladiators' shields. But if you are determined to use a historical setting, you must be even more hyper-vigilant about consistency and never let your scenery wobble.

> 'Ada Goth sat up in her eight-poster bed and peered into the inky blackness. There it was again. A sigh, soft and sad and ending a little squeak. Ada looked across the bedroom as she held up the candle and stepped out of bed.'

This quote is a great example of how to give a illustrated children's book a historical setting. The text tells us that Ada is living somewhere special because her bed has posts on it. And not just four of them, but eight. So it must be somewhere special, and large. When she reaches for a candle and not a light switch, the text tells us she is somewhere special, large, and in a period where electricity wasn't available. No reader has been bashed around the head with this information. It is seamlessly woven into our introduction to the character of Ada and her Byronic-era life. And it is done via that golden rule again, that backbone of good storytelling: *it has been shown, not told.*

Chris Riddell has the advantage of both writing and illustrating *Goth Girl*. Having set the scene with these carefully selected words, he goes on to give the reader a beautifully detailed map of Ghastly-Gorm Hall. Words and pictures share the storytelling just as they are supposed to.

Key idea

Even if you don't have the luxury of illustrating your own work, the rule still applies. Show more than you tell, keep the aspects of your setting memorable but brief, trust an illustrator to see you right on the finer details, and never let any of your scene-setting slow down the forward motion of your plot.

FUTURISTIC/FANTASY SETTINGS

This one is tough, too, because you have to imagine so much of it and you don't have many words with which to do it. There aren't many futuristic books aimed at a younger audience, perhaps because of the level of world-building required. On a more positive note, the only limit on a futuristic setting is your own imagination and the imagination of your illustrator. It's much the same with a fantasy setting. Purple moons, weather systems that produce custard-flavoured rain: you can have them all! However, you must remain aware that your readers will need reference points. If your setting is devoid of anything recognizable, how will your readers be able to place your characters within it? Give us something to anchor ourselves to in the midst of the weirdness. Too much weirdness translates badly, particularly for children.

CONTEMPORARY SETTINGS

In a contemporary setting, you don't need to write so much about your surroundings to bring everything to life, because we all live in a contemporary world. But you still need nuggets of information to position your characters. And don't assume *everyone* knows about contemporary things you take for granted. I remember once talking to a fisherman in a remote part of Scotland who found it incredible that you couldn't walk down Oxford Street in London without constantly having to adjust your stride in order to avoid other people. If you are a city dweller writing about city life, the underground trains, large department stores and multi-ethnic crowds that are part of your everyday experiences will feel exotic to someone living in deepest Wales – or, indeed, urban Africa. Be sure to inject your contemporary world with a sense of place: the stink of diesel fumes or the press of people. Use your eyes, ears, senses: all the material you need is around you. Just be sure to pick out the interesting details, not the humdrum.

Write

Describe the place where you live in one brief paragraph. Keep your description as factual as possible.

Look again. Are there any small details you missed? One odd-coloured brick, a drainpipe that goes nowhere, a certain smell, the feel of the door handle under your fingers? Add those details to your description.

How many of your original observations now feel unnecessary?

What to include and what *not*

When you are adding details to your setting, make sure that you include any elements you want to feature in the plot. If there is an ornate key in the door which you want the reader to remember because it has a crucial role to play later on in the book, make it visible. But don't be heavy-handed about it. Tuck it into a conversation, or a brief aside. Make sure that it features in the illustration. Your reader will remember it when the time comes.

Equally, if there are lots of details that interest you but don't add anything to the story, leave them out. It's tempting, if Victorian locomotives are your thing, to go on at length about trailing wheels and crank axles and the fragility of cast-iron connecting rods and forget that your story is supposed to be about the passengers on your train, not the train itself. Your characters and plot must always remain in sharp focus. If your setting is taking over from your characters, backtrack and prune.

Place as mood

Ghost stories are frequently set in deserted houses covered in cobwebs. Happy stories more often take place in sunny meadows than abandoned factories. The choice of a setting can create the mood for any story you want to tell.

Let's drop a character into a spooky castle. The walls are pressing in on him, and there is a smell of rot and rats. He meets a locked door and doesn't have a key. The place is ganging up on him, building a mood of menace.

Using different places in the same story can create contrasting moods. The impact of a story that moves from a sunlit riverside to a dank water tunnel is much greater than if that story were to take place in just one spot. The Dursleys' house is fussy, neat and unremarkable where Hogwarts is vast, unpredictable and exciting. The places are well described, but it's their juxtaposition that gives them their potency.

Weather, light and time

'It was a dark and stormy night...' These are the opening words of Edward Bulwer-Lytton's 1830 novel *Paul Clifford*. Madeleine L'Engle used the same words to open her avant-garde 1962 children's novel *A Wrinkle in Time*. The phrase has become shorthand for the kind of purple prose best avoided when setting a scene – unless you are prepared to use it ironically as Madeleine L'Engle does. Like it or loathe it, it encapsulates the way that weather can be used to affect mood. You can heighten drama with judicious use of thunderclaps, or make a scene dreamy and calm with spring sunlight dappling through leaves. A sunny day suggests a happy story; a howling gale implies a thriller. It's a useful code, and should be embraced – with a weather eye, as it were, to clichés like Bulwer-Lytton's.

If you are feeling adventurous, you could try clashing your weather with the mood you want to convey: louring skies as the hero triumphantly finds the treasure or bright sun at tragic news. But this takes skill and practice and you may find that it sits uncomfortably unless you know how to use the contrast to enhance what's happening. Use whatever feels right and don't force whatever feels wrong. If it feels wrong, it probably is.

" Janet and Allan Ahlberg, *Funnybones*

'In a dark, dark town there was a dark, dark street and in the dark, dark street there was a dark, dark house and in the dark, dark house there were some dark, dark stairs and down the dark, dark stairs there was a dark, dark cellar and in the dark dark cellar.... Three skeletons lived!'

The Ahlbergs' classic *Funnybones* sets the scene with its rhythmic use of the word 'dark'. It fits the characters of the skeletons and builds the anticipation. Within one page the scene is perfectly set. The illustrations, with their consistent use of black, match and enhance the mood.

Time can be used in the same way as light. Twilight, with its sense of the known and the unknown coming together; dawn, with its promise of newness; the soporific sense of a hot summer's afternoon. Use these tools with abandon. Don't just make it a sunny day because you like sunny days. Have reasons. The lower the word count, the more important those reasons become. Remember those bold lines. If it's hot, make it so hot that your character's bicycle wheels melt into the tarmac they way they do in Rome in August. Show, don't tell. Make your reader shiver and sweat alongside your characters. Do this and your work will sing.

Place as catalyst

Places can act not just as backdrops to the action but as catalysts. If you find your story faltering, consider moving your characters to a fresh place. You might find a change of scene gives your plot fresh impetus. A fresh setting can often provide what's needed to keep your plot moving. The Pevensey children find Narnia in the back of a wardrobe; Harry Potter finds Diagon Alley behind a combination of bricks in the yard of the Leaky Cauldron.

Moving from place to place

If you are moving your characters around, be clear in your own mind where they are going, and where this new place is in relation to the original setting.

Changing backgrounds – even if you're just moving characters from room to room – require explanation, and explanation can slow a plot down. Ask yourself: how much information do we need? Must we know that the character got off her chair, walked across the carpet, turned the door handle, pushed open the door, blinked and saw... whatever she saw? A lot of books that I edit fall into the trap of characters standing, turning this way and that, bearing right down a corridor and left up some stairs... yawn... I don't need this level of logistical detail. It should be implied in the forward motion of what you are writing.

A plot always needs this sense of motion. A detailed exposé on which bus Ernie and his fellow earthworm friend Boris take to the dance hall for the competition, which streets they pass and what conversations they have on the way might be physically moving the characters along and passing the time, but it's doing nothing for the plot.

 Key idea

A real bus journey may take half an hour, but it should take only a couple of lines in your story. Books are designed to take us out of reality, and should always give us the interesting stuff instead of the mundane. Isn't that why we read them?

Ditch the meandering. Prune the random conversations. Cut it all back as savagely as you might an overabundant plant. Trust your readers. They will know that the characters haven't leaped in the blink of an eye from Ernie's wormhole to the dance hall without you having to spell it out for them.

Maybe there are details of the journey that you deliberately want to include. Why do you want to include them? Do they further the plot? Do Ernie and Boris meet someone important on the way, do they pass something that will directly affect the narrative arc? If the details have no bearing on the plot, get rid of them. By all means have their bus route clear in the privacy of your head – props to you for some thorough world-building – but leave any decorative details to the illustrator. You may find that the only sentence you need is: 'Half an hour later, Ernie and Boris arrived at the dance hall.' You may find you don't even need that.

Using line breaks

Writers often circumvent this need to explain how a character moves from A to B by using a line break: a line of space in the middle of a piece of text. A line break isn't as strong a cut-off point as a chapter break, but it's stronger than a new paragraph. It firmly shows that one scene has ended and another has begun, usually elsewhere. It's a useful shorthand for moving your characters from place to place in the quickest possible way. You simply leave Ernie and Boris in the wormhole discussing choreography, have a line break, and pick up the story in the dance hall. Job done.

When to describe setting

This might be more easily described as when *not* to describe setting.

Don't spend ages at the beginning of the story describing where the action is going to take place without any action to go with it. If you bore your readers with topographical details and peculiar weather patterns and no human interaction or plot development for more than one or two paragraphs, they will put your book down before your characters have made an appearance. No one invests in scenery. Be single-minded about hooking your readers with a character or an exciting scene, then reel them in with those little orientating touches.

Don't describe a place at the height of any action. When Ernie and Boris are in a tense dance-off against a talented, multi-legged spider (I'm liking the potential of this story more and more), the reader doesn't want to know what the floor or windows of the dance hall look like, or the name of the town, or what the weather outside is doing. And don't waste time describing a place after the action has occurred, either. It's too late by then. Your reader wants to move on to what happens next.

I am now picturing you all staring forlornly at a spinning, rainbow-coloured roundabout in a playground. You want to jump on but can't see how to do it. If you can't set the scene before the action, during the action, or after the action, when do you set the scene?

Telling stories is never about scene-setting/action/character development/emotional input in strict sequential order. It's about reducing all aspects into one delicious morsel. Or, as novelist and screenwriter Chuck Wendig puts it: 'Find ways to let the snake bite its own tail.' Wendig makes a parallel with the junk-food industry when talking about writing. When you eat a doughnut, you aren't thinking about proportions of salt, sugar and fat: you're thinking about the fantastic taste on your tongue.

Focus point

You need to mix it all in together. Trick the reader into not noticing what you're doing. Give them something delicious, moving forward all the while. Spin the roundabout fast enough and let the colours blur into white.

Aim to drip-feed the sense of place as the story unfolds. This keeps the pace up, the plot moving ever forward. We rarely need to know exactly where a character is in the very first sentence. How the character is feeling in that environment is always more important than where he is.

> 'Ernie and Boris waited nervously as the dancers lined up and the judges arrived.'

This sentence doesn't mention the dance hall. It doesn't have to. The reader can see where Ernie and Boris are, thanks to the mention of dancers and judges. Having seeded this, we can then move on to giving the readers a more physical sense of place.

How you do this is another case of using 'Show, don't tell' in your writing. Compare the following:

1 'Ernie and Boris were in the dance hall, looking at the judges.'
2 'The light coming through the dance hall windows was so dazzling that Ernie couldn't tell if the head judge was a grasshopper or a dragonfly.'

The first sentence *tells* us where Ernie and Boris are. The second *shows* us. By seeing the scene through Ernie's eyes, the reader will get a much stronger sense of place, just as by showing a character's personality in the way they speak and act makes that character more vivid.

Two sides of the story

Let's assume that you've created your world and written your text and got a publishing deal. (Insert cheer here.) Your editor will now suggest an illustrator. It won't be you, unless you are a qualified artist with exactly the vision that the editor is looking for. It won't be the friend you lined up to illustrate your story unless s/he, too, is a qualified artist with exactly the right vision and so on. It will be who the editor decides it will be. If you hate the idea of handing over the reins of your lovingly crafted story to a total stranger, then I'm afraid the world of children's publishing will be a shock to you. Publishing illustrated books is a collaborative thing, not an exercise in massaging one person's vision into existence.

If you really hate the choice of illustrator and can explain why in reasonable tones, say so. But I would advise you to let yourself be persuaded. Publishers and illustrators know their business. You may find your story acquires a whole new facet you could never have imagined.

Contrary to popular belief, it's rare for writers and illustrators to work together. Usually the text is written and the pictures are added, or vice versa. Chris Riddell believes that keeping the writer and illustrator separate is a healthy and exciting way of producing illustrated work because you just don't know how the illustrator's vision will add to the writer's. Of course, as both writer and illustrator, he has had the luxury of both writing and drawing his Goth Girl series exactly how he wanted it to be.

When you work with an illustrator, it's important to remember that places and characters may end up looking quite different from how you imagined them. That's part of the fun. Don't be precious. Don't dictate everything in your text, just those elements which are vital to the progression of your plot. Let the illustrator find their own way to tell the visual side of the story. Trust them. They are professionals. You don't question why an electrician wires your TV in a certain way. You just let them do their job. Let the illustrator do theirs.

Workshop

For this workshop, I would like you to return to the story you plotted out in the Workshop at the end of Chapter 8 and to think about the setting or settings. Ask yourself some questions:

- How important is the setting to the story?
- Does the plot necessitate one or multiple settings?
- What role will time of day or night play in the story? And how about weather?
- How will you reveal the setting to your readers?

Next step

In the next chapter we will look at voice, and how to find your own style. We will look at points of view and relatability to the audience, how to keep your voice consistent and how to avoid the snakepits of cliché and overwriting.

10

Voice

A lot of first-time writers worry about this nebulous thing, this 'voice', this unique style the world expects them to create. They look at the competition, they mimic what they see, they cram their sweaty fingers around an ill-fitting pen and grimly wonder if they're doing it right.

Award-winning author and illustrator Emily Gravett spent a long time trying to find a voice – a style – that she thought people wanted. And as a result, she received mixed feedback on what she was producing. It was only when she thought, 'I'm going to create what *I* want to create' that she found her voice had been there all along. She just had to let herself be herself.

Chuck Wendig

'The writer's voice is the thing that marks the work as a creation of that writer, and that writer only. You read a thing and you say, "This could not have been written by anybody else." That is voice.'

Developing an individual voice

A book full of printed words isn't the best place to demonstrate an illustrator's voice. Dig out and study for yourself the work of illustrators such as David Tazzyman with his spiky, scribbly images, Lauren Child with her colourful collages or Axel Scheffler with his quirky squirrels. You will see how individual they all are, like a bookshelf full of fingerprints.

Author voices are more easily demonstrated here. Take a look at the examples below:

> All ready to put up the tents for my circus. I think I will call it the Circus McGirkus.

This is, of course, Dr Seuss of *The Cat in the Hat* fame. His voice is one of the most recognizable in children's fiction, particularly when paired with his iconic cartoon illustrations. In his writing, he often used the terrifyingly named 'anapestic tetrameter' – four rhythmic units of two weak syllables followed by one strong one – with a strictly limited vocabulary for early readers, plus the odd (I use this word advisedly) made-up word.

> Four red apple noar me chair – who so careless put them there?

This is taken from Valerie Bloom's counting book *Fruits*. Her strong Caribbean voice bounces off the page with its use of patois, rhyme and rhythm. A good poet will have voice in *spades*.

> Look out! Rollo Rabbit's steamroller has run away. Crunch! Crunch! CRUNCH! It has squashed three cars flat.

Richard Scarry's voice takes the form of interactive conversation with the pictures in his book *Cars and Trucks and Things that Go*. It's simple and confiding. His voice makes him – and you by extension as you read his stories aloud – as much a part of the story as what is on the page.

I'm not showing you these examples so that you can rush off and copy them. Emily Gravett made that mistake on your behalf. I'm showing them to you as proof that there are as many different author and illustrator voices out there as there are authors and illustrators. Your voice is as distinctive as you are, and should evolve naturally as you develop your stories. Don't force it. Tell the story you want to tell, in the way you want to tell it. That is your voice, for better or worse.

 John Geddes

'If you want your own distinctive voice, you first have to become someone.'

Sometimes you can cheat a little. If you have created a really good character, that character might take on the role of 'voice' on your behalf. This voice can vary from book to book, just as your characters do.

When I was working as an editor, I once received a letter, sample chapters and outline of a young adult (YA) manuscript from a teenager named Jack Curling, introducing his story. The author Mark Swallow had let his main character approach the publisher and do the talking. (It turned out that Mark had form as an adult author, having won a Betty Trask award for his book *Teaching Little Fang* in 1991, so he knew what he was doing. Don't use his story as evidence that you too should circumvent the normal rules in this way.)

When you write stories in the first person as Mark did, you put yourself into that person's shoes and speak as they do. This is something actors recognize, any innate shyness disappearing as soon as they step into a role. Many of them find acting a role easier than living their own lives. Many authors feel the same when it comes to writing.

Even if you are telling the story in the more distant third person (I'll get to the distinctions between different points of view shortly), you can take a short cut by creating a narrator to take charge of the 'voice' for you. Lemony Snicket, narrator of the book series A Series of Unfortunate Events with illustrations by Brett Helquist, is a construct by the author Daniel Handler for exactly this purpose. Lemony Snicket opens the first book in the series, *The Bad Beginning*, with the following words: 'If you are interested in stories with happy endings, you would be better off reading some other book.' The voice is one of lugubrious despair and foreboding that warns of disaster at every turn and gives a distinctive flavour to the books. Daniel Handler's own voice is more modern, realistic and pitched at an older level, best seen in his young adult writing.

Point of view

Before we go any further, let's talk about point of view (POV). What is it? And how can writers use it? I do mean writers here. Writers have to be aware of different points of view and how to use them when they write. Illustrators aren't usually faced with having to make point-of-view choices. They always get to play omniscient narrators, as described below.

FIRST PERSON

First-person POV delivers the story from behind the eyes of a witness to events: 'I went', 'I was thinking' and 'It happened to me'. There is a thrill to it for the reader, who gets the chance not just to follow someone else's story, but to *be* someone else as well.

First-person POV in picture books is rare, although it can work if you keep the narrative voice as close to a small child's viewpoint as possible, as Rod Campbell does in his classic *Dear Zoo*. It's important to remember that young children are just starting to work out that they separate beings within their family units, so telling them that they are someone else can puzzle more than enlighten. When you factor in pictures as well, it can get even more confusing. Imagine telling a story in the first person, where you have an illustrated rabbit as the main character. The exchange between the adult reader and the listening child would undoubtedly go something like this:

'Hop, hop, hop, I'm going to nibble some grass—'

'Mummy, I don't like eating grass.'

or:

'You always say I will be sick if I eat grass.'

or:

'Daddy, I ate some grass, like the rabbit in the book…'

Occasionally in picture books you will find first-person plural, 'we', as in Michael Rosen and Helen Oxenbury's classic *We're Going on a Bear Hunt*. Here, the 'we' character is a family. The plural

POV in *We're Going on a Bear Hunt* is inclusive and comforting as 'we' tiptoe through a cave and wake a sleeping bear together. I can't imagine the book being nearly as much fun to read if you're expected to do it all by yourself. 'I'm going on a bear hunt, I'm going to catch a big one...'

First person can also be tricky for young fiction. Newly independent readers battling through the brambles of early literacy can struggle to put themselves in characters' shoes when they have so much else to contend with already. At this level, I've never seen the exclusive use of 'we'. The longer the book, the more the reader needs to invest in the main character – and a generic plural 'we' is never going to generate that kind of investment.

First-person POV really starts making a serious appearance only once you get into middle-grade fiction. Tom Gates, Greg Heffley and Barry Loser all tell their own stories to great comic effect. But it really comes into its own in young adult fiction, where it's very much in vogue at present because of its immediacy. The thrill of being someone else is well suited to teenagers as they experiment with where they fit in the world.

The challenge with a first-person voice is how limited you are. You can see the story only from your chosen narrator's perspective, and other people's thoughts and ideas are closed to you. You, the storyteller, have to keep your thoughts to yourself and let your character do the talking instead – rather as Mark Swallow did with Jack Curling. The moment you take a short cut via someone else's eyes, the spell breaks. We have no idea what other people in our real lives think and know; why should your character be any different? Remember this basic rule of life and apply it to your first-person writing.

 'The Diary of the Dark Lord' (astoldbyvoldemort.tumblr.com)

'Dear Diary. I was showcased in the Opening Ceremonies of the London 2012 Olympics today. I feel quite honored, but who is this Mary Poppins chick? And why were there 500 of her? These are the questions that will haunt me forever. Love, Voldy.'

The diary format is a popular way to approach a first-person narrative, evidenced most famously by Greg Heffley, the main character in the middle-grade classic *Diary of a Wimpy Kid*. Liz Pichon's Tom Gates series is also written in diary form, heavily doodled throughout because the character thinks very much in pictures (a great character quirk that immeasurably enriches the books). It's a terrific way into a character's head, putting the reader bang in the driving seat. However, in a dated diary, the main character will be going through events in real time without the benefit of hindsight – unless s/he opens a diary to recap on what's happened so far. And be realistic when considering the age of your narrator. A six-year-old wouldn't have the literacy skills for diary writing.

You need discipline to use a first-person approach. If the treasure is behind the wall, your narrator has to go the long way round to find it, unless they have extendable legs like Inspector Gadget and can peer over the wall for themselves. They can't see through the wall either, unless you have given them special powers to do so. (If you do give your characters powers, don't make the mistake of revealing those powers only when you need them. That is the way to losing your readers' trust. Flowers don't appear from nowhere; they have to grow from seeds.)

Key idea

With first-person POV, you must be directly involved in all the action; you can't witness anything happening elsewhere; you may need to rely on other people to tell you what's going on.

If you do use information from other people to further your plot, take care not to turn your first-person narrator into a passive cipher for all the important stuff happening elsewhere. Judge how important the information is, then give your narrator the right weight of responsibility for it to keep him/her at the heart of the action. Remember: the main character must ultimately be the master of their own destiny.

It can be comforting to work inside first-person limits once you understand them, because your story can move only in one direction. However, it's very easy – particularly for first-time writers – to make the mistake of sliding sideways into lots of different points of view. This mistake invariably dilutes the story you are trying to tell.

When using first person in children's books, you also have to remember what age your main character is. This might be anything from six to 16 years old (see Chapter 1). Unlike in adult fiction, you cannot write as yourself in the first person, unless you are genuinely six or 16. There is not only a vast difference in life experience between those ages and your own, but there is also quite a gap between the six-year-old and the 16-year-old themselves. This knowledge must inform the voice you use.

Let's take a look at how you the adult, the six-year-old and the 16-year-old might perceive the same situation. Imagine that you are all members of a family that is about to get a dog. You will probably have different reactions along the following lines:

'I can't wait!'

'Whatever.'

'I hope it doesn't poo on the carpet.'

It's not hard to work out which age would have which reaction.

You should also be thinking about your characters' *physical* line of vision, especially from an illustrative point of view. Children see the world from considerably lower down, which affects scale and perspective. Roald Dahl used to lower his 6-foot 6-inch frame to the ground and crawl around on his hands and knees to get a better sense of the world from a child's point of view. I recently hoisted up my own nine-year-old, to demonstrate where his adult line of vision might end up. He gazed at the kitchen he's known all his life in astonishment. Putting yourself in the same position as your readers in this way will make your characters more relatable to your audience.

Children don't always notice the same things as adults. Sometimes they fail to notice things you assume are unmissable. I am a prime example. When I was three years old, I went to New York with my family. I remember Bloomingdale's and Father Christmas, and I remember my little brother's balloon popping beneath the wheels of his buggy. If I were to illustrate a picture book about a three-year-old in New York, an image of the popping balloon would resonate strongly with my own three-year-old sense of the world far more than a beautiful picture of the Empire State Building. (Apparently we went up the Empire State Building. I have no memory of that at all.)

THIRD PERSON

A third-person viewpoint – 'he ran', 'she was thinking', 'it turned out', 'they didn't do it' – is perhaps more familiar, particularly at picture-book level: 'A mouse took a stroll through the deep dark wood...' Third person gives more distance than first person as the reader stands back from the story and observes.

Third person can be broken into two categories: close third-person and the omniscient narrator.

Close third-person works almost like first person, except that you are telling the story perched on your character's shoulder rather than inhabiting their head. You are Long John Silver's parrot. Your viewpoint is a little wider than first person, in that you can turn your head in that special parroty way and see what's going on around you more than the person whose shoulder you are borrowing, but you still can't read the minds of others. The mouse, for example, has no idea what the fox or the owl or the snake might be saying to each other while he is chatting to the Gruffalo.

As an **omniscient narrator**, on the other hand, you know it all. You hold everything in your hand like a pen-wielding deity on Mount Olympus. The power can be dizzying, the opportunities endless. This is particularly true for illustrators, who can pick and choose exactly what a reader will see regardless of viewpoint (other than occasionally bearing in mind the eye-line of the reader). But it can also overwhelm unless used with care. If you flit too much from viewpoint to viewpoint, from start to finish and back again, you are likely to end up with thin, unrelatable characters – and, if you read the chapter on character carefully, you will understand why this is a Bad Thing. Flitting is no good unless there is a great deal of action to distract you. And too much action – as discussed in the chapter on plotting – usually means that the characters aren't getting the attention they need in order to come to life on the page.

Relatability

🗨 J. D. Salinger

'What really knocks me out is a book that, when you're all done reading it, you wish the author that wrote it was a terrific friend of yours and you could call him up on the phone whenever you felt like it.'

Your voice has to relate to your audience. It has to resonate like a bell, harmonize with the tune already playing in their heads. Your readers want to feel as if you are their best friend, that they can tell you anything and you'll understand. Successful children's authors get letters from their fans all the time that ask for advice and guidance as much as they ask about plots and characters. These authors have found that all-important way into their reader's minds and hearts by telling their stories in ways children feel are just for them. Empathy should always be at the heart of your voice when creating children's books.

Bear in mind at all times the age of your readers. This will also add to the relatability of your voice. Ten-year-olds the world over recognize elements of themselves – the way they speak and act, the way they feel towards teachers, friends and siblings – in the Tom Gates books. This is why Liz Pichon has been so successful.

Don't be afraid of using difficult vocabulary, though. If you are careful with it, it should enhance your readers' enjoyment and understanding of the story you're telling. Don't, however, throw around tough vocabulary unless you have laid a legible trail towards the meaning of the words you have chosen. Ted Hughes's story *The Iron Man* encapsulates this in its opening page.

> The Iron Man came to the top of the cliff... He swayed in the strong wind that pressed against his back. He swayed forward, on the brink of the high cliff.

The opening line places the Iron Man at the top of the cliff: simple words, strong image. With this picture in mind, the child can then approach a word like 'brink' further down the page and make an educated guess as to its meaning.

'[Children] are more sophisticated than they are given credit for,' says Alex T. Smith, author-illustrator of *Claude*, 'and more than capable of latching on to and understanding quite complex ideas. I think it's much better to get a child asking questions than them understanding every single word.'

Overwriting

Steve Maraboli

'The volume of your voice does not increase the validity of your argument.'

Like a yell in a lift, an overwritten voice should be avoided for the sanity of all concerned. Take a look at the following.

'I had the bestest time <u>ever</u> in the whole entire world!!!!' said the little girl in a happy voice. 'The jellies were my most *favouritest* flavours in the universe!! I got the <u>coolest</u> presents!!! My dinosaur outfit was the MOST DINOSAURIEST OUTFIT at the entire party!!!! Thanks, Mum, for giving me such AMAAAAAZING party!!!'

Children can and do talk like this. But this level of shouty excitement doesn't work when you write it down. This is because the eye is distracted by all the exclamation marks – known as 'screamers' in the publishing trade – italics, underlines and capital letters. The whole thing is visually overwhelming, and the visual overload distracts from the story. A good story shouldn't need this many visual props. The words and actions should generate the voice all by themselves.

Take a look at this alternative version:

'I had the BEST time,' squealed the little girl, jumping up and down. 'The jellies were my most favouritest flavours in the universe. I got the coolest presents. My dinosaur outfit was the most dinosauriest outfit at the entire party. Thank you, Mum, for giving me such an amazing party!'

Exclamation points and words in capitals are kept to the minimum. Instead, the girl's excitement is conveyed by the word 'squealed' and by the way she jumps up and down (a great example of 'Show, don't tell'). The reader isn't visually distracted.

Visual language

When you are writing illustrated stories, you might want to bear in mind that your reader isn't the only person you're trying to enthuse. You want an eager illustrator, too, someone who can't wait to leap into the energetic word pictures you're painting and join in the fun. Compare the following:

1 The little dog barked loudly and chased its tail.
2 The tiny dog gave a booming bark and chased its tail in crazy circles.

The second sentence has more visual cues than the first. A tiny dog will get an illustrator's mind working harder than one that is merely little. The contrasting sound of its bark might also trigger ideas in the illustrator's mind, as will the energy of the phrase 'in crazy circles'. Make the words you use interesting.

Coherence

What you will find at first, if you try to force a voice that isn't naturally yours, is that it will peter out as your story progresses. You might, for example, start a story about princesses with all the familiar tropes of the fairy tale: 'Once upon a time…', thees and thous, 'good Sir' and 'my lady queen' and so on. You may then become so engrossed in your story that you forget you've placed it in this kind of time and place, and start using modern phrases that don't fit with the rest. Pick an approach and stick with it. This is also true of your illustrations. Don't start a story with an intricately detailed picture, then get sketchier as you go along. It looks unprofessional and disturbs the flow of the story you're trying to tell.

Rhythm and rhyme

Rhythm is critical in picture books and young fiction. These are books designed to be read aloud, whether by a parent to a child at bedtime or a child to his or her teacher at school. You must never allow your words to plod.

A classic plodding error is a repetitive sentence structure. My personal bear trap of a structure is this: 'Something happened, allowing something else to happen.' For example: 'Ernie looked at Boris, wondering if his friend could dance.' This may be tighter than 'Ernie looked at Boris and wondered if his friend could dance' and can speed up a sentence. But, used too often, it loses its power. Catch yourself early. Mix it up. Use short sentences for exciting, snappy action, and long sentences for contemplative description. J. K. Rowling often uses ellipses in her most dramatic moments: 'This happened... that happened... something else happened...' The ellipses give the jerky effect of drama all happening at once.

Curiously, any events that happen in a flash – the casting of a magic spell, the leaping of the monster from behind the tree – are those events that need to be given time in a book. Use short sentences, but use lots of them. Build your pictures and whip your audience into a frenzy of anticipation. Don't let the climax be over in as long as it would take in real life. Let your reader savour the moment, millisecond by millisecond.

Focus point

Slow down in the fast bits and speed up in the slow bits.

Equally, those long drawn-out moments of hanging around at a bus stop or waiting for a late-running parent should be skipped over. Everyone knows the feeling in real life. They don't want to feel it in a book. They want to get to the exciting bit, and then they want the exciting bit to last as long as possible.

Other methods of introducing rhythm into your writing are to use word tricks. Alliteration is always great in picture books: 'The crafty crocodile crept along…' Onomatopoeia for picture books lends itself to fun, imitative fonts. Use inventive metaphors and similes that surprise. Try a rhythmic beat in the style of Dr Seuss, or strong rhyme like Julia Donaldson.

If you attempt rhyme, I can't emphasize enough how strict you have to be with yourself. *Every single part* of your rhyme must work. There can be no weak links. Never force a rhyme just because you want to use the word 'canary'. Never try to squeeze in a sneaky extra syllable because you can't see how else to do it. If it isn't working, you have to kill it and start again. There is no other way. In the words of Cressida Cowell's Viking Hooligan tribe, 'Only the strong can belong'. Rhyme is extremely exposing, and anything less than perfect will get you chucked on the editorial bonfire.

Clichés

Clichés should be avoided like the plague.

Imagine the first person to use that expression. Someone must have been the first. I bet they felt really proud when they came up with it. Wow! Plague is hideous! Everyone will gulp and shrink away from the thing I want to tell them to avoid. It's genius! Maybe it was in 1666. It's not any more.

Andy Stanton makes up wild similes in the Mr Gum series such as 'as guilty as an onion', which both convey what he's trying to say and give him a distinctive voice. Being a writer gives you an opportunity to break away and approach your descriptions with a fresh eye, ear, nose and throat. Think of it as coming up with clichés for the future.

Chuck Wendig

'Voice matters. Voice is important. But at the end of the day, if it takes your story and drowns it in a hot stockpot of scalding soup, then you've done yourself a disservice.'

Workshop

For this workshop, I would like you, first, to look critically at three children's authors, perhaps taking in two or more of their books in each case. Compare and contrast, then write a paragraph about each author's voice. Finally, I want you to do a piece of your own writing and, as honesty as you can, consider whether you have an individual voice. How distinctive is it? Could it be *more* distinctive and how could you achieve that?

Next step

In the next chapter we will look at the vital tools of the writer's trade: parts of speech, punctuation, conventions of dialogue and the use of speech tags.

11

Grammar

Illustrators, look away now. I am going to talk about words for a while: specifically all the different parts of speech and how we put them together. Language is the only tool that writers have to tell their stories. It is the well-oiled, finely tuned machinery beneath the bonnet of your sleek and shining Rolls-Royce of a tale. Poorly used language kills stories. Too many words, words used in the wrong context, words that are too difficult or too easy for the readership, overlong sentences, the use of five words where one will do – all these are language crimes. Mastery of the language you use will equip you far better to tell the stories you want to tell than if you just wing it.

An awareness of appropriate grammar levels is vitally important when writing for children and their widely varying reading abilities. It's also invaluable to know the correct terminology, or all those conversations you have with an editor in your heady published future will be as clear as mud.

Nouns and proper nouns

Nouns are *things*. They often follow *the* (definite article) or *a/an* (indefinite article): a child, the end, an earthworm. They are countable: three wombats, seven dwarves, a hundred and one dalmatians – although you will come across what are known as uncountable nouns, too: time, money, love. (Uncountable nouns often have a countable alternative: hours, coins and kisses can be counted but time, money and love can't.) Proper nouns are the capitalized names of things: Ernie, London, Old Father Time.

Nouns are the agents of your story. They act, or are acted upon. Your characters are nouns. So are their possessions, their pets, their families and all the objects they encounter. Without nouns, there is no *thing* for the story to happen to. There is no cat to illustrate, no orphan to find a home; no home, indeed, for the orphan to find.

Nouns can be *subjects*, which means they are actively doing something. Ernie the earthworm likes line-dancing: Ernie is doing the liking. They can also be *objects*, which means they are having something done to them by another noun. Boris helps Ernie. Ernie isn't doing the helping; Boris is. Boris is the subject, and Ernie is the object.

Pronouns

Pronouns are the words substituted for nouns when you don't want to repeat the noun. Like nouns, they can be the subject or the object of a sentence. Unlike nouns, however, they change their form depending on whether they are subjects or objects, providing hours of fun for students studying English as a Foreign Language.

- **Subject pronouns:** *I/you/he/she/it/we/they*
- **Object pronouns:** *me/you/him/her/it/us/them*

There is also the useful **possessive pronoun:** *mine/yours/his/hers/its* (rarely used)/*ours/theirs*. For example: 'The oddly shaped gerbil is mine.'

This/that/these/those can be used as subject and object pronouns, too, if used in place of a noun: 'Can I have that?' *Something* is another word that can function as a pronoun if used in this way. Question words are pronouns, too. *Who...?* = a mystery person (i.e. a noun). *What...?* = a mystery object, i.e. a noun. *Where...?* = a mystery place (i.e. a noun). And so on.

Here's a quote from *Bogwoppit* by Ursula Moray Williams and illustrated by Shirley Hughes, demonstrating the use of pronouns:

> The bogwoppit, if *this* [a bogwoppit] is what *it* [a bogwoppit] was, came flopping and shuffling into the room, leaving a damp trail of webbed footprints which Samantha instantly recognized, because *she* [Samantha] had seen *them* [the footprints] that morning on the top of the cellar stairs.

If you use *this/that/these/those* but keep the noun in the sentence – as in 'that morning' from the quote above – the words *this/that/these/those* slide down the pecking order of importance to become **determiners**. There is a similar group of words denoting possession – *my/your/his/ her/our/its/their* – which look like pronouns but aren't, because they must be used with nouns: my earthworm, his gerbil. This makes them determiners, too.

You probably don't need to know this stuff in such detail, but I love the nitty-gritty of grammar. I'm fun at dinner parties.

Verbs

Where nouns and pronouns are *things*, verbs are *doing words*. The infinitive of a verb is always written 'to [doing word]': to line-dance, to laugh at grammar jokes. If you're unsure whether a word is a verb, try to break it down to the point where you could put the word 'to' in front of it: I have been running = 'to run'.

When using verbs, you have to think about which tense to use. As we are looking at children's books, we can probably leave the future perfect progressive out of this, and focus on present and past tenses.

The present tense is most often used when narrating books for very young children. Here is the entire text from a reading-scheme book called *Splash!* which I wrote for Collins Big Cat:

> I can see clouds. / I can see rain. / I can see umbrellas. / I can see a puddle. / SPLASH! / Now I'm wet.

It's not very interesting language, but it's doing its job: teaching a child to read using the present tense together with simple vocabulary, simple sentences and plenty of repetition to reinforce what the child is learning. It also gives the illustrator ample opportunity to share the storytelling. The sentence 'I can see a puddle' isn't spoken by the main character, a little girl out for a walk, but by the little girl's mother, who has seen the puddle where the little girl hasn't.

Present-tense narrative is going through a fashionable phase with teen books at the moment, offering an extra immediacy for readers aged 12-plus. Otherwise, it's most often seen in dialogue, as in this extract from Ursula Moray Williams's *Bogwoppit* again:

> 'You can have any room you please as long as you keep it tidy and stay away from me!' Lady Clandorris conceded. 'Can you cook?'
>
> 'Oh yes!' said Samantha, 'I can cook.'
>
> 'Then you can look after yourself,' said her Aunt Daisy with relief. 'I eat very little myself – mostly spinach and herbs and things out of tins.'

The past tense is the most common tense used in children's books for narrative and description. It's so familiar that it hardly needs explaining; except to say that the simplest past tenses (I went / he was line-dancing) are more suited to the younger end of storytelling than the more complicated past tenses (I have been crying / I hadn't thought of that). Take a passage from the young series-fiction book *Ellik the Lightning Horror* (Beast Quest 41):

> A patch of mist broke apart and Tom glimpsed a strange, blue glow among the trees. He saw rainbow-coloured fins flickering on a long body that slid along the ground, curling and knotting around the mangrove roots.

Compare this to the more complicated tenses used in the 12-plus fiction book *Boys Don't Knit* by Tom Easton:

> At some point, I suppose I'll have to tell Dad my secret. He's not going to like it, especially the fact that I've been lying to him for so long, but this can't go on. Tonight was the closest I've come to being caught red-handed.

Active and passive voices

The main character in *Boys Don't Knit* is Ben Fletcher, aged 17. In the last sentence of the paragraph above, he talks about 'being caught red-handed'. This is the **passive** voice. Ben isn't doing the catching; his dad is. An **active** voice is where the character is responsible for the action: Ernie is line-dancing. A passive voice is where the character is on the receiving end of whatever's going on: Ernie *is helped by* Boris, Ben *is caught red-handed by* his dad.

The passive voice looks like this:

Is / was / is being / was being / has been / had been

[helped, caught, etc.]

[by someone or something]

Boys Don't Knit is for older readers with a wider grasp of these subtleties of tense and voice. In young fiction and picture books, that grasp isn't a given. It could even make the difference between a child turning the page in your book or putting it down as too difficult. In young fiction and picture books, your characters need to be as active as possible. This seems obvious advice, given that your characters will be driving your story. But it's amazing how many first-time writers make the mistake of using a passive voice instead of an active one. From the point of view of an illustrator, who wants to draw a character who isn't doing anything?

 Key idea

If good text should flow like a river, the passive voice is the kink in the current when the river hits a boulder. It's clunky. It uses three words instead of one. It's sneaky, pretending to put the character in charge by making them the subject of the sentence – then taking away all the character's power. It's tough grammar to grasp. Try not to use it in text for young readers.

This doesn't mean that your main character has to do everything. Boris *can* help Ernie. Boris, the subject of the sentence, is being active. As long as Boris doesn't steal the limelight from Ernie in the overall narrative arc, he can help as much as he likes.

Contractions

These are not the ones you have in hospital, but the ones where you reduce two words to one, using that famous little troublemaker, the apostrophe. I could spend paragraphs on the apostrophe. For something so small, it causes no end of trouble.

The word 'apostrophe' comes from the Greek. According to *Merriam-Webster's Collegiate Dictionary*, it means 'the addressing of a usually absent person or a usually personified thing'. In other words, something's missing.

In the case of contractions, this meaning fits perfectly. When *I have* becomes *I've*, the letters 'ha' in 'have' are removed and replaced by the apostrophe. *Do not* becomes *don't*, the 'o' in 'not' replaced by the apostrophe.

Occasionally you see contractions that are wrong: *do'nt*, for example, or *theyv'e*. If you understand that the apostrophe replaces a missing letter, you should be able to avoid making such mistakes.

Listen to conversations around you. You'll hear contractions everywhere: *I'll, we've, doesn't*. Spelling the words out – *I will, we have, it does not* – can feel odd and formal unless they are used this way on purpose. Lola from Lauren Child's *Charlie and Lola* sometimes avoids contractions, as in 'I will never not ever eat a tomato.' The gamblers in the 1950 musical *Guys and Dolls* combine the informality of slang with the formality of never contracting phrases. This is their style, their voice, and very effectively used to identify a particular culture.

> HARRY THE HORSE: I just acquired five thousand fish.
>
> NICELY NICELY JOHNSON: Five thousand? If it can be told, where did you take on this fine bundle of lettuce?
>
> HARRY THE HORSE: I have nothing to hide. I collected the reward on my father.
>
> BENNY SOUTHSTREET: It is an advantage to have a successful father. Nobody ever wanted my old man for as much as five hundred.

Remember, however, that early readers need to be able to read those original structures – *I will, they have* – before they can tackle contractions.

Possessive apostrophes

When apostrophes are used to denote possession, people seem to struggle. I don't know why. The rule is simple. When a noun (an earthworm) or proper noun (Ernie) is singular, put an apostrophe at the end followed by an 's'. The same applies to a plural noun that doesn't end in an 's', like 'children'.

> One earthworm's ballroom mission.

> Ernie's love of line-dancing

> A children's book

When a word is plural and already ends in 's' – as most English nouns do – put the apostrophe at the end by itself.

> Two earthworms' dream

Never use apostrophes for plurals (*apple's and orange's*). Only use an apostrophe in 'it's' when contracting 'it is' or 'it has'.

Remember these basic rules and you will make an editor very happy.

Adjectives and adverbs

 ## Roald Dahl

'Eschew all those beastly adjectives…'

 ## Stephen King

'The road to hell is paved with adverbs.'

Adjectives and adverbs are *describing* words. Adjectives describe nouns, whereas adverbs describe verbs – so you might have a *red* ball or a boy who runs *quickly*.

It's tempting to use lots of adjectives and adverbs when you begin writing. You want your audience to understand exactly how you're seeing something. However, beware heavy-handedness. Too many describing words will kill a description more quickly than bug spray will a bug.

When it comes to adjectives, remember that your illustrations will be doing most of the descriptive work. What is the point of *telling* your audience that the ball is red, and then *showing* the audience that the ball is red? This belt-and-braces approach adds nothing extra. If the fact that the ball is red is a fundamental aspect of your story – the colour is magical, for example – then you should mention it in your text. But if it's just there for the reader to visualize, let the pictures do the work.

More interesting, perhaps, might be a story where the words and pictures deliberately *don't* match. Your text might state: 'This is a red ball.' Your picture might then show a blue ball. Immediately, your story is greater than the sum of its parts. Of course, you'll have to build in an explanation if your pictures actively contradict your words. But the point remains an important one: don't describe things if a picture could describe them better.

Write/draw

Write a short story (300 words) about a red ball. Illustrate it with a blue ball. Why don't the words and the pictures match?

Adverbs should also be discouraged. While your pictures may not be able to describe verbs quite as easily as they can nouns, you have the whole of the English language at your fingertips to do this kind of illustrating for you.

Let me demonstrate:

1 The boy ran quickly.
2 The boy sprinted.

These sentences mean the same but the second is better because 'sprinted' means both 'ran' and 'quickly'. You have made your sentence sharper and more interesting by finding a verb to represent both the doing and the way that it is done. (You don't need to sprint quickly, by the way. This is tautology: the use of two words where one will do.)

You must of course bear in mind the age of your readership. Don't use complicated verbs at every turn just to show off. Your story must serve its reader. Make that child sprint, but if you are unsure whether your reader knows the word, make sure that you have planted enough clues along the way for your reader to work it out. If the context is strong enough, a child will work out what you mean.

Snapshot

Find more interesting, descriptive verbs for the verb-plus-adverb structures below.

- Angus ate the doughnut greedily.
- Billy lay lazily on his bed.
- Lizzie spoke angrily to Angus.

Dialogue

Having addressed the idea of using dialogue to build characters, let's take a look at it now from a grammatical point of view.

It fascinates me how different languages punctuate dialogue, because that's the kind of party girl I am. In French, you either get funny little sideways double 'V' shapes («…») framing the dialogue or no quote marks at all, leaving it to the em-dash (—) to indicate when someone's speaking. Swedish and Finnish both use what I would call closing quote marks (') at the start of dialogue as well as the end, plus a cheeky little comma outside the quote – an English grammar crime.

In English, quote marks can be either double or single: 'dialogue' or "dialogue". In both cases, the marks face in opposite directions, bracketing the dialogue that you put inside them. Double quote marks are more common in picture books and young fiction; single quote marks predominate in middle-grade fiction upwards. All punctuation that is part of the quoted text should be *inside* the quote marks, as should a comma when the quote is in a sentence with a speech tag. For example, this is seen in my Space Penguins book *Galaxy Race*, aimed at five- to eight-year-olds:

"This baby is faster than a rocket with a rocket up its bottom," Rocky boasted.

USING SPEECH TAGS ...

Rocky the rockhopper penguin 'boasted'. He could have just 'said', but 'boasted' shows an important element of Rocky's character in this scene, where he is showing off his new spacecraft to a crowd of admiring onlookers.

'Rocky boasted' is a speech tag. It indicates how a piece of dialogue is said, and who is saying it.

Any verb that demonstrates the act of speaking can be used as a speech tag. Using words like 'laughed', 'smiled' or 'winked' as speech tags ('You're looking lovely today, Ernie,' Boris winked) is cheating, because none of these verbs has anything to do with opening your mouth and making sounds. Use 'he said with a grin' or 'she told him, laughing' or similar structures instead.

Using a simple 'he/she said' is fine, by the way. In fact, it's actively encouraged, especially at the younger end of illustrated fiction. Legendary US writer Elmore Leonard famously uses nothing else, and he writes for adults. Too many 'he gasped', 'she groaned', 'they yelped' can distract the eye as much as too many exclamation marks.

The only problem with 'said' is how easy it is to fall into the adverb trap when using it: 'he said dramatically', 'she said awkwardly'. I could easily have used 'said proudly' instead of 'boasted' in the quote above. J. K. Rowling likes using adverbs with 'said' speech tags in the Harry Potter series: the only things I struggle with when I read the books.

Adverbs undeniably have their uses. I would just advise moderation and clever thinking. Whatever your character is saying, you should try to make it sound awkward or dramatic in its own right. If you do it right – if you strike 'show don't tell' gold – that adverb will be redundant. A very big plus point indeed.

...BUT NOT TOO MANY

You've hammered out your dialogue and are feeling happy with who says what. Now look again at what you've written. You don't need as many speech tags as you think. If the conversation is clear enough and moving along at a good pace, you can often get rid of 'he/she said'. But do make sure that you start a new paragraph whenever someone different is speaking.

'Can you do a pirouette, Ernie?' asked Boris.

'Sure I can. Watch this.' [said Ernie.]

CRASH!

'Did you crash into the wall on purpose?' [asked Boris.]

'Of course I did. I do everything on purpose.' [said Ernie.]

It's clear who's saying what even without the speech tags in square brackets. Mentioning Ernie's name and Boris's name once in the first line is all that's needed.

This is an example of where any work you have put into your character development can help clarify who is speaking. I have written the characters here so that Ernie sounds bossy and over-confident while Boris sounds slower and in need of reassurance. Because the personalities are so different, I don't need 'Boris said' or 'Ernie said' more than once to be able to follow the conversation.

Instead of a speech tag, you can sometimes cheat:

Boris hurried over to Ernie. 'Did you crash into the wall on purpose?'

Boris here is clearly the speaker because he is the subject of this fresh paragraph. No speech tag required.

You want to be a little careful when using people's names in dialogue. I feel as if I have told you this a thousand times already in this book, but *everything in moderation*. Boris uses Ernie's name once in the conversation above. It's common for first-time writers to overcompensate in dialogue, constantly repeating the name of the person their character is talking to in case the reader doesn't get it. Have a little faith. In real life, you don't repeat a person's name every time you address them. It sounds odd.

International language

Be aware of the words that you use when you write, particularly if you are writing picture-book text. To stand a chance with publishers, resist regional and culture-specific words with all your power. Keep your images translatable as well. The perfect picture book appeals to as many different cultures as possible, to maximize co-editions and make that bottom line profitable.

Workshop

This workshop is simple... and possibly a challenge as well. How good – or how bad – is your grammar? Even those of us who think we have mastered every grammar point out there have in reality something to learn. Go to the library or bookshop and borrow or buy a good book on grammar and make up for your shortfalls. It will be worth it, I promise.

Next step

We will look at dialogue next: how people speak versus it looks on the page; the lazy use of dialogue as 'filler'; reported speech and thoughts; how to avoid clunky dialogue and maintain consistency; and how to convey more than just words through conversation.

12

Dialogue

The Russian-American writer Vladimir Nabokov famously disliked dialogue. This may have played a part in his writing once being criticized as containing 'the clatter of surgical tools'. Dialogue, particularly in children's books, helps readers empathize with characters through their conversations. Dialogue develops character, plot, pace. It breaks up long passages of narrative. It can reveal and conceal vital elements in your plot. Fundamentally, it *communicates.* 'Dialogue is the place where books are most alive and forge the most direct connection with readers,' says American YA fantasy author Laini Taylor. 'It is also where we as writers discover our characters and allow them to become real.'

David Hare

'The actual business of writing dialogue is not thought of as a craft.'

How people speak

Chimamanda Ngozie Adichie

'I write from real life. I am an unrepentant eavesdropper and a collector of stories. I record bits of overheard dialogue.'

When was the last time you eavesdropped? If you had taken down verbatim what you'd heard, might it have looked like this?

'Um, yeah, I need the thing, it's, like, the thing that, well, you use to, er, do the thing...'

I have several conversations a day along these lines. I'm sure you do, too. It's how people speak. But it makes no sense by itself. It needs all those other conversational cues that you get when you are face to face with someone: a pointing finger, a glance, a shared reference, an in-joke.

In books, you don't have the luxury of these cues. All the reader has to go on are the words printed on the page, plus as much sense of what's going on in the narrative as you can give them (always showing, not telling, of course). As a result, dialogue in books will always be a little bit fake. But you still have to make it sound real. How do you do that?

'I need the thing,' said Lizzie.

Billy rolled his eyes. 'What thing?'

'That thing,' said Lizzie.

This is essentially the same conversation as the one I am always having with my children. The difference is that I have turned it into written dialogue.

Firstly, I have removed all the stammers and non-words – *um, er, yeah, well, like* – plus their attendant commas. People do speak like this all the time, but all of these tics are visual stumbling blocks in dialogue. The eye gets so snagged in them that the meaning is lost.

When writing picture books, cut them out entirely unless a well-placed 'er...' is fundamental to your plot. Every single word in a picture book needs to earn its place, because you have so few to work with. Don't use them in reading-scheme books or any book aimed at early readers. Those readers are already struggling with what they have, so don't confuse them with unnecessary 'um's or 'well's. Even right up to longer middle-grade books, you should think twice about using these non-words unless you are doing so to illustrate, for example, the nervous speech of a character or to maximize uncertainty at a given moment in the story. Don't use them if they serve no purpose.

The second thing I've done is to divide the dialogue between two speakers. By introducing a second speaker, you are starting a *conversation*, which is immediately more interesting than a monologue. You should never let one character waffle on for more than a paragraph at a time. That is a lecture, not a piece of dialogue, and no one likes listening to lectures. A conversation, on the other hand, offers all kinds of storytelling opportunities: red herrings, vital clues, misunderstandings, all of which can open up your plot.

Of course, we can't leave the redesigned conversation as it currently stands. Because we are telling a story, the 'thing' needs to be explained. Where a conversation like this might tail away in real life with no explanation ever forthcoming, in a book you will always have to clarify what the thing is. Otherwise why mention it?

'I need the thing,' said Lizzie.

Billy rolled his eyes. 'What thing?'

'That thing,' said Lizzie, pointing at the TV remote.

Don't be afraid in dialogue to commit all those grammar crimes drilled out of you at school: contractions, unfinished sentences, phrases that don't link together as smoothly as they might had the speaker had a chance to polish them first, vague words where specific ones would be more accurate, incorrect question words. Technically, Billy's 'What thing?' above should be 'Which thing?', for example, but who speaks like that nowadays? Dialogue isn't the place to impress upon your readers the niceties of grammar if it doesn't reflect a realistic conversation. No one thinks about what they are going to say before they say it to quite *that* degree – except perhaps Mr Collins in Jane Austen's *Pride and Prejudice*.

> ## Write
>
> Record a short conversation between you and a friend (or friends, if you are feeling ambitious). I don't need to tell you to ask their permission, of course.
>
> Next, transcribe it as accurately as you can, including all those non-words I mentioned above.
>
> Finally, rewrite the conversation as you might like to see it in a work of fiction.

Dialogue as filler

The next thing to establish is the importance of that conversation between Billy and Lizzie. Why do we need to know that she wants the TV remote? Is it a pertinent fact, or an illustration of character, or is it just filler?

In real life, people can happily chat about nothing for hours. Not so in books. Your dialogue can't be filler. It has to serve a purpose. It needs to demonstrate a personality, establish a plot point, move the story forwards. Nothing is drearier than what American novelist Edmund White calls 'coffee-cup dialogue', where speakers are interchangeable and nothing happens. For example:

'Can you pass the biscuits?' asked Alex.

'Here you are,' said Lizzie.

'Can I have one?' asked Billy.

'Of course you can,' said Lizzie.

'Mmm,' said Alex. 'Chocolate biscuits are my favourite.'

'I prefer Hobnobs,' said Lizzie.

What is the point of this exchange? Does a crucial plot point rely on Lizzie's preference for Hobnobs and is this is your sneaky way of establishing that? Do you need to take so long about it? Could it have been more swiftly established in a narrative form?

While the boys wanted chocolate biscuits, Lizzie preferred Hobnobs.

Short and sharp – job done. You haven't given your readers' attention a chance to drift. By using waffly dialogue, all you are doing is filling the page and bringing that brisk pace you've been working so hard on to a grinding halt. Make your dialogue earn its keep. It needs to be a lean, mean chat machine.

 ## Focus point

Speech and thought bubbles are useful when writing short, heavily illustrated text because they can be sprinkled into the heart of your illustrations to highlight particularly important pieces of dialogue. Speech and thought bubbles have to be exquisitely short, because there is very little space for anything but the most essential words.

Composing a speech or thought bubble is a perfect exercise in cutting dialogue back to the bone for any writer. It's worth attempting if you find you have written a piece of dialogue that feels long and unfocused.

Show, don't tell

 ## Michel Hazanavicius

'When you're with your wife, you don't say I love you to your wife every day but the ways you look at her and your actions are another way to communicate. Don't focus on dialogue, only focus on what you're expressing.'

Michael Hazanavicius is the director of the Oscar-winning silent movie *The Artist*. Having successfully told a fully fleshed-out story with just a few subtitled words, he's interesting on the subject of how to use dialogue: essentially, what he is telling us is that we shouldn't put the onus on the dialogue to tell our reader everything. Use your dialogue to say a few things, but back up the details with other indicators, like the way your characters are behaving as they speak.

'I love line-dancing,' said Ernie.

Boris twirled across the room. 'Me too!' he cried.

Boris has *told* us he loves line-dancing in the dialogue. He has also *shown* us that he loves line-dancing in the narrative. This is an example where showing *and* telling can enhance your story. Add an illustration showing Boris's happy face as he twirls, and your reader can't fail to hear what you're saying.

You can play around with the effect if you're feeling mischievous. Why not make your characters say one thing, but behave in such a way that it's clear they don't mean a word?

'I love line-dancing,' said Ernie.

'Me too,' said Boris, gazing longingly out of the window at the football stadium across the road.

This is a rich seam to explore for that important element in your plot: conflict. Perhaps Boris isn't that into line-dancing, after all. Perhaps at the last moment, he has to make the call between a free ticket to the football and the line-dancing final. The conflict ratchets up the drama and the pace of your plot. What will Boris decide?

Don't, however, show and tell *too* much. Beginner writers often feel the urge to explain what a forthcoming piece of dialogue will be about before their characters speak.

Lizzie decided to tell Billy she wanted the TV remote.

'I want the TV remote,' she said.

They think they are preparing the ground. They are preparing nothing but a singular urge in that reader to put the book down. All dialogue needs to be able to pack its own punches.

Dialogue and character

Nicholas Cage

'When I act, I hear it like music. In my head, I hear the dialogue like music.'

Many illustrated books are designed to be read aloud to a young audience by obliging adults. Your dialogue needs to be interesting, convincing, characterful and perhaps even a little bit tuneful. If you are writing the voice of a monster, you want to invite the reader to use a monster voice. You want to encourage interaction and drama. Great dialogue should make you want to put on a special voice to do it justice.

If you have developed different read-aloud voices for your characters, you have developed aspects of those characters for your readers. Dialogue is great for fleshing out the personalities of your story: whether they speak fast or slowly and the phrases they use. My redesigned conversation above, for example, illustrates two things about my characters: Lizzie's vague way of talking and Billy's clear exasperation.

 Roddy Doyle

'I see people in terms of dialogue and I believe that people are their talk.'

Good dialogue enhances character not just by what your characters say but how they say it. In David Walliams's *Mr Stink*, illustrated by Quentin Blake, Mr Stink is an aristocratic tramp. The heroine Chloe asks him if she can buy him a bar of soap. His aristocratic side shows through as soon as he speaks. It makes the reader want to use that voice when reading his dialogue aloud.

> 'Thank you my dear. But I have no use for soap. You see, I had a bath only last year. But I would love some sausages. I do adore a nice meaty sausage.'

The use of phrases like 'my dear' and 'I do adore' makes Mr Stink gentle and posh. David Walliams could simply have told us that Mr Stink was aristocratic in the narrative – and he does – but backing that up with dialogue makes the old tramp's personality much more vivid.

Andy Stanton's Mr Gum is another great example of character development through dialogue. This dirty old man is cruel and rough. His dialogue backs this up, dropping his 'g's off the end of words (horror!) and using distinctive made-up words (something that is much harder to pull off than you think).

> 'Shabba me whiskers! Who'd've thought poisoning that stupid whopper dog could be such hard work? What a bother it all is.'

Meanwhile, Polly, the heroine in *Mr Gum*, speaks with passion, often uses long breathless sentences and has a distinctive accent that is impossible to read 'straight'.

> 'I loves that dog, watch out cos it's true! I loves him and what's more, that dog saved my life once and now I'm not gonna stand by playing in a hedge while that old grizzler flippin' poisons him to death and destruction! No way, says I! I'll stop him, that's what I'll do!'

This is a case where lots of exclamation marks are acceptable because they are part of the vocal flavour. These examples make the characters sing with rhythm and interest. Aim for the same.

Snapshot

Choose books by one two of your favourite children's writers and write a 500-word 'compare and contrast' report on how they handle dialogue, focusing especially on its relation to character.

Focus point

Take care not to go overboard with accents or pronunciation. Just a few strange words sprinkled here and there will work. Otherwise, as with too much punctuation or too many 'non-words', you confuse the eye and slow down the storytelling. There are some classic authors who used heavy dialect, such as Frances Hodgson Burnett with Dickon in *The Secret Garden*, but modern readers are less tolerant of the time it takes to decipher. Everything in moderation should see you right.

Reported speech and thoughts

Reported speech is when dialogue is turned into description, without the quote marks or the sense of immediacy that a conversation brings. For example:

> Lizzie told Billy that she wanted the thing, and Billy didn't know what she meant so he asked her, and she pointed at the TV remote.

This has the effect of distancing the reader from what's going on. If you can put the words into the mouths of your characters, do it. Occasionally, reported speech is useful for recapping a previous conversation that the reader already knows about, but be sparing with it. And avoid it altogether if writing a short text. You want to keep your reader in the moment.

In writing, thoughts are a form of dialogue inside a character's head. Thoughts should have the same immediacy, rhythm and interest as dialogue when read out loud. They can, of course, be represented with a thought bubble in pictures.

Clunky dialogue

Avoid the situation where your story is flowing nicely, your reader is visualizing everything and anticipating what happens next... when suddenly there is a piece of bad dialogue: a clunk that doesn't fit, like Dick Van Dyke and his cockney accent in *Mary Poppins*. Dialogue like this:

'Hi, Mum. Hi, Dad. I'm going to the shops. I'm buying a lolly. I'm getting a newspaper. I'm seeing my friend later. I'm going to be late for school.'

The rhythm is repetitive and dull. The content is worse. The dialogue tells us nothing about the character, except that they are boring. If your dialogue is as stilted as this, you pop the fictional bubble.

Consistency

Carl Hiaasen

'Lots of people can write a good first page but to sustain it, that's my litmus test. If I flip to the middle of the book and there's a piece of dialogue that's just outstanding... then I'll flip back to the first page and start it.'

The sign of an amateur writer often lies in the inconsistency of their writing, whether in dialogue or narrative. If you have a character who speaks in a certain way, make sure that they speak in that way from the start of your text to the finish. Don't let your characters blur into one another and all sound the same. Don't let characters lurch from well spoken to rough and uneducated without good reason. Aim to distinguish your speakers throughout. Don't rely on your illustrations to do the distinguishing for you. There's a job to do in the text as well.

Workshop

What was the last conversation you had? Can you remember the content? Write it down. Try to have at least four lines of dialogue.

- Take out any non-words: *um*, *er*, *like*, *well* and so on.
- Attribute what's being said to a speaker with the simple speech tag 'he/she said'.
- Check your punctuation. Are the quote marks in the right place? Is all the punctuation inside the quote marks?
- Was the conversation resolved? If not, resolve it in your own imaginative way, or add some extra dialogue to open the way to some kind of plot development.
- Add narrative to describe the way the characters are acting as they speak. Are they smiling or frowning? Is there any fidgeting? Do their actions match their words?
- Are the speakers distinct from each other in any way? Could a reader tell who is speaking if you removed the speech tags?
- Practise reading your dialogue aloud. How does it sound? Are you doing 'a voice'? Are the sentences too long? Too bumpy with commas and pauses? Too repetitive? Are you adding drama, are you moving the plot along?

Next step

In the next chapter we will be looking at the process of editing. We will revisit all those aspects that we have looked at so far – character, plot, setting, voice, dialogue, grammar – and challenge ourselves to improve on them. We will also consider the art of cutting, as well as the importance of good presentation.

13

Editing

You've finished your first piece of writing. Well done! You should be pleased. Vast numbers of would-be writers simply never finish their great idea, and then wonder why no one has ever discovered their genius. If you've got a story with a solid plot and well-fleshed-out characters that you have managed to write from beginning to middle to end, loose ends tied up, a sense of images in place, that is half the battle won.

But only half.

Now the real fun begins.

Now it's time to rewrite the whole thing.

If this idea makes you groan and lay your head on your desk in a state of sheer refusal, then I'm so sorry. It can't be helped. Write, then rewrite, then rewrite again. I've recently finished a project that I must have rewritten five times. It took two-and-a-half years, from discussion to publication, and it wasn't even illustrated. To paraphrase Bette Davies, writing books isn't for sissies.

66 99 David Fickling

'P. G. Wodehouse contains in his butlers nearly all the editorial advice a good editor will ever need.'

Editing is tough...

It's tougher than writing sometimes. Writing is where you're in the flow of the river, immersed in your world, thrilled by the genius flashes of your pen and your miraculous turns of phrase. What a simile! What a joke in a million! What an expression on the face of that squirrel! It's energizing, where editing is sapping. It's balm to your creative soul where editing is salt in the wound.

Man up, troops. You've finished a piece of work. You owe it to yourself to make that piece of work as good as it can possibly be. You think it shines now? You wait until you have pruned it. It's going to be *gorgeous*. But it's also going to be painful.

Anthony Browne, the UK's Children's Laureate from 2009 to 2011, poses the question: you have a video camera and the instruction to video your life for 24 hours. Then you have to edit 24 hours to 1. What would you leave in? What would you take out? If you think in terms of a film, your story will be the better for it.

John Irving

'Half my life is an act of revision.'

Character

Samantha Shannon on Twitter

'Just did a search and boy, are my characters doing a lot of pausing in this book.'

How many characters have you chosen? I'm guessing you have one main character and a few minor ones. Any more than ten and you want to consider your reasons for including so many in what will be a short book.

Let's think about your main character first. Are they clear in your head? If you're still fuzzy on motivations or eye colour, your readers won't believe in them. They are entirely dependent on you to make this character as real to them as they are to you.

Did you make a list of character attributes for your main character before you started writing? If you did, now is a good time to cross-check with your finished piece of writing for consistency. If your character no longer matches your list of attributes, that's OK. You're allowed to change your mind; nothing needs to be set in stone as long as you are *consistent* about your changes. The main thing is that your character rings as true in the middle and end of your story as at the beginning.

Dorothy Parker

'I can't write five words but that I change seven.'

Review the physical aspects first. Do they still have the blond/brown/red/colour-of-choice hair you envisaged? Is that dimple on the right cheek still present? Can you clearly picture what they are wearing? In picture books it's not worth changing your characters' outfits unless the plot demands it: you want a clear code for your readers that the girl in the green dress at the start is the same girl in the green dress at the end. If they were tall at the beginning of the book, make sure that they are still tall at the end. These details all matter, particularly in illustrated books. Take the time to iron out any physical fuzziness.

What about movement? Has the limp the character had in Chapter 1 mysteriously disappeared in Chapter 5? Are they suddenly the fastest runner in school, have they magically learned to swim without explanation where previously they were too scared to dip their toes in the water?

Look at their family members. Did they start with a brother and end up with a sister? Do their parents look the same at the end as at the beginning? Have they changed any aspects of their personalities with no explanation? Every change needs to be the result of what has gone before.

Names can often trip up an author. Has someone changed names midway through the story because you decided you preferred Molly to Milly? Have you never quite decided how to spell Siobhan? (Point of order: not the greatest name to use for young readers because it is impossible to work out the sound via phonetics.) Spell-check on a computer is extremely useful for these blanket checks and changes. Your character could be virtually three-dimensional, but one slip from Sammy to Sonny and the scenery will fall flat.

So much for consistency. What about change? While certain aspects of your main character need to be consistent, the best stories have a main character who learns something about themselves through the course of a book. Remember what I told you about character arc, and how important it is that your character should be forged through the fire of the story. Have they learned anything about themselves at the end of the story, or has the whole thing been a meaningless exercise in moving from A to B?

Once you have reviewed your central character, look at the secondary ones, too. As I said at the beginning of this section, if you have more than ten you should question what they are all doing in your story. Successful picture books rarely have more than two or three characters to identify with; young fiction may have a few more. Why dilute the story with characters who do nothing but prop up the furniture? Cut them out. If you're particularly fond of them, give them a reason to stay.

Key idea

Secondary charcaters can be there only if they have something important to do, on which a plot turn will in some way depend – It's not enough simply to involve them in a piece of dialogue that has no bearing on the plot – whether it's the weather or a taste for Hobnobs. Line 'em up, knock 'em down. Who's valuable enough to stay on your team?

Edit

Go to one of your own stories (even if you are only halfway through one) and review it in the light of the *characters* only. Try to ignore any other issues during this edit.

Plot

Take a look at your narrative arc first. Does it have the three vital components of a successful plot: movement, pace and conflict? If you had to sketch a graph of your plot, would it have plenty of rises and falls, with the highest spikes occurring towards the end? Would that graph look like the kind of roller coaster that would be fun to ride?

Have you set the scene, outlined the problem, resolved the problem? Can you take it a step further and break it down into the three-act structure? If you did this work before you started writing, you should find that it still works at the editing end. If, however, you changed aspects of the plot as you went along, has it affected the structure in adverse ways?

 Bop It audio game

'Do it again. But better.'

THE BEGINNING

We're back in the car park again. This time, you mean business. And, crucially, you have hindsight. You know how you reached the castle. You know about the tiger in the side-street. Now you are going to strip out all the dead weight that you accumulated as you blundered about the car park looking for the exit. You are going to sharpen this knife of a beginning until it could cut the page it's printed on.

Firstly, look out for repetition. I frequently get into a groove of using the same expressions; when I come to edit my work, they jump at me like fleas. Keep one, but only one. Two if it's a really, really unobtrusive expression. No more than that.

Ask yourself serious questions about all those adjectives you have used to set the scene. Do you need them all? Are they are crucial factor in your story, or are they just padding? Can they be covered by the illustrations, or demonstrated in the action? Cut, cut, cut.

Look carefully at your adverbs now. Can you tighten up your writing by getting rid of all the 'happily's and 'excitedly's? Find verbs that express what you mean in one go.

Time to ask yourself some tough questions. How many cars are necessary for your backdrop? Which details can be dealt with in a picture? Can you leave that car park any faster?

Focus point

Often, first drafts get into their stride by the second chapter, not the first. Ask yourself: if you cut out the entire first chapter, will the story still be able to stand up? Which crucial details do you need to get the story going?

Anton Chekhov

'My own experience is that once a story has been written, one has to cross out the beginning and the end. It is there that we authors do most of our lying.'

THE MIDDLE

Is the middle feeling tired? If your story flags at this crucial stage, you'll never build up the momentum you need for that that final roller-coaster ascent that prefigures your ending. If you feel bored rereading it, so will your reader. Cut any scenes, characters or dialogue that serve no purpose. Everything that happens needs to happen for a reason. Remember that magic number three? Rise and fall, rise a little further and fall a little further, rise the highest of all – three times maximum for books this length, I would advise – then cruise across the finishing line with the full weight of your momentum behind you. There's no time to smell the flowers or take endless photos of that dog sunbathing under the bench.

THE END

Does it satisfy? Will your reader put the book down with a sigh of pleasure or a growl of frustration – or, worse, a shrug of the shoulders? Please don't tell me it was all a dream. Is the ending totally irrelevant to what went before, did you just end it because you were bored? Question yourself relentlessly. If you have a surprise twist, make sure that there were enough clues scattered in advance either in the text or the illustrations for your reader not to feel utterly confounded. You want them to frown, then go 'Ah, so *that's* why the tiger came out of the side-street!' All loose ends must be tied up. Use what you have, don't embellish as an afterthought unless you're prepared to go back through the story with a fine-toothed nit comb and insert a suitable number of references so that your embellishment feels real. You must end happily. All your characters must have played their part. No exceptions.

 Chuck Wendig

'I … am constantly seeking those opportunities to use the LEGO pieces I already have rather than seeking out new ones.'

Edit

Take the same piece of writing you looked at in the previous 'Edit' exercise and review it in the light of the *plot* only, giving consideration to the beginning, the middle and the end. Ignore any other issues during this edit.

Setting the scene

Consult your map if you have made one, and do the same with your setting as you did with your main character: check for consistency. The Town Hall needs to be in the same place at the end as it was in the beginning. Check addresses: don't have a bungalow where previously you had a house. If you have a historical setting, double- and triple-check your facts. If it's sunny on one page and rainy on the next, be sure that a) the change of weather is relevant or b) stick with one or the other. Watch out for timings, too. Do your characters move through believable days and nights? Does it *matter* if it's day or night? A change of light can add interest to your illustrations, so it may be worth while from a visual point of view. But the action of the plot should be far more interesting than whether it's four in the afternoon or two-thirty in the morning.

Be particularly careful when you move from place to place that your writing doesn't get leaden. Don't stand, turn, wait, move, stop, start again. Boring. Get your characters from place to place *quickly*. Thread their movement through with plot-propelling dialogue and asides about the flowers in the park that they are driving past: don't dedicate pages and paragraphs of description to bus routes. Let the pictures describe the scene as far as possible.

Key idea

Remember the doughnut: give readers deliciousness, not ingredients. Use line breaks. Keep moving in a realistic direction.

Edit

You know the spiel. Take your piece of writing and review it in the light of the *setting* only.

Voice

What tone are you using? Did you start out humorous, then forget to tell the jokes? Do the illustrations get darker and more sinister while the text gets lighter and funnier, or vice versa? Is there a reason for this mismatch? Be clear in your own mind whether your book is a funny book with serious bits, or a serious book with funny bits. It can't be funny and serious in equal measure, because each aspect will dilute the other and you will end up with something indifferent. I wouldn't advocate seriousness from start to finish for this age group: leaven your story here and there to give your readers breathing space.

Focus point

Have you been shouting in the lift where you should have been whispering in the cave? Rein in that punctuation and trust the power of the plot to do the telling for you.

Does your voice match your audience? Three- to five-year-olds won't enjoy anything too highbrow; older readers hate to be patronized. Don't assume children won't get big ideas; just take care how you write them.

Is your point of view consistent? If you are telling the story from the first person, does the text ever leap mysteriously into the mind of the other characters? Tidy it up. Are you writing in the present or the past tense? Have you used that tense consistently, from start to finish?

How is the rhythm of your text? Have you varied your sentence lengths, have you written in the most visual language you can muster? Have you got pages of description or dialogue that need breaking up and mixing around? Have you avoided clichés like the plague?

Edit

You've guessed it: take your piece of writing and review it in the light of the *voice* only.

Grammar and spelling

Are you still shaky on where to put your apostrophes? Is all your punctuation *inside* your consistent double or single quote marks? Check, check and check again. If you rely too heavily on your computer to tell you where you've made mistakes, you will still find errors creeping in: 'bare' where you meant 'bear', 'their' instead of 'they're': spelled right, but wrong in context. Read your story with care and take responsibility for your own mistakes. It's the safest way to catch as many as you can. No one expects a manuscript to be entirely free of mistakes; editors know that you're human. But do your very best to catch at least 99 per cent of your errors.

Don't assume that the story is good enough to dispense with basic spelling. You're hoping to show your work to editors, whose lives depend on apostrophes and who can debate whether the verb 'to smooth' has an 'e' on the end for *hours*. Presenting badly spelled work to editors is like stepping on to a trawler and announcing that you can't be bothered with fish. It's plain bad manners.

> ## Edit
>
>
> For this one, I would like you not only to review your piece of writing for the quality of the grammar and spelling but to give it to someone else you trust to do this as well.

Dialogue

Does your dialogue sound convincing? Age-appropriate? Have you been ruthless with all those non-words like 'um' and 'well' and 'like'? Have you converted dreary monologues into lively conversations? Does your dialogue illustrate your characters and move the plot along at the same time? Does every word earn its place, or is it just chitchat keeping the page warm?

If you are using speech bubbles, speech tags aren't necessary. If you want to use different fonts to indicate different speakers the way Liz Pichon does in her Tom Gates books, adding visual interest, speech tags are also redundant. If you're using conventional dialogue, look again at exactly how many speech tags you need to keep the conversation as clear and flowing as a chalk river. Try to cut back to one or two speech tags per conversation. If it doesn't work, think a little harder about the quality of your dialogue and how you can convey who is speaking without using a speech tag. Bear in mind how much work your illustrations will be doing for you.

> ## Edit
>
> Back to you only for this one. Review your piece of writing in terms of *dialogue* only.

Raymond Briggs

'Fast running seems to turn into flying quite naturally. Snowmen are made of snow which floats down from the sky, so going up there again seems natural.'

Words versus pictures

I hope that, by this stage in the book, bearing illustrations in mind throughout the process of writing your story is now second nature. This part is all about double-checking. How much detail do you need when describing that car? How essential is it to your plot that the little girl's shoes are yellow?

If you are planning to illustrate as well as write, do you have pictures that flow naturally from the text, or are you forcing images because you like them? Do the pictures do a job, or are they merely filling space?

Edit

Finally, review your piece of writing in terms of the *balance of illustration and text* only. Of course, you may very well not have any actual illustrations to hand at this point, but you need to have at least an idea of what will be shown and what not.

Margaret Atwood

'A word after a word after a word is power.'

Presentation

You have checked plot, character, dialogue, setting, every full stop, comma, double letter and silent 'g' in your text. Now that your actual writing is in the best shape it can be, it's time to look at how to present it so that other people can read it.

If you have handwritten your text, I'm afraid you will need to type it up. Handwritten manuscripts are unprofessional and difficult to read. Unless your handwriting is part of the visual appeal of your story, type it out.

Use A4 paper. Use a readable font. Don't try to jazz up your story with an informal font like Comic Sans; you'll make enemies, not friends. Always double-space the lines so that each page of text doesn't overwhelm the reader. Use one side of the paper *only*. Using both sides works in books, but reading a story on A4 paper is a completely different experience. No strangely coloured, strangely shaped paper, no gimmicks, no flourishes. No free chocolates inside the envelope. Your book must stand on its own feet without any enhancements.

Key idea

If the text is good enough, it will shine through the simplicity of the presentation. Anything fussier suggests that you are trying to hide something. Let your text speak for itself. The frills and folderols can come later.

Tim Wynne Jones

'Adult novels are about letting go. Children's books are about getting a grip.'

Cut!

Recently, I edited a book down from 80,000 to 50,000 words. Thirty thousand words gone, but the plot still firmly in place, clearer and sharper than before and a hundred times better.

If your heart breaks at the thought of deleting 30,000 words in one go, try putting them to a file named 'extra text'. Chances are, you won't want to put them back again – but it's comforting to know that you *could*. You can revisit the material at a later date, and perhaps fashion a new story out of what's there. The same thing applies to illustrations. Just because you made the brave decision not to use them at this time doesn't mean they can't be used at a future date. Nothing needs to be wasted.

You do need to know when to stop, or there won't be any book left. Think again about your market, and the length of book you're aiming for. If you started a project as a 40,000-word middle-grade fiction story and you ended up with a straight-talking 8,000 words, you may have a problem. You may also, of course, have transformed a mediocre middle-grade book into a perfect, precision-cut piece of young fiction. If the story works well at a quarter of its original length, then perhaps your *métier* isn't where you thought it would be. Feel your way. You'll soon discover the point where you can't do any more.

Tautology

A great word which means 'using two words where one will do'. A quiet silence is an example of tautology. No one wants to know about 'very unique' items, or 'frozen ice', or 'an evening sunset'. Be strict. Make every word count.

Ernest Hemingway

'Prose is architecture, not interior decoration.'

Workshop

No book is perfect, even a published one, so it can be an interesting and enlightening process to critique a published children's book in the light of the editing stages outlined above. One way to do this would be to make enlarged photocopies of every spread (for a classic 32-page illustrated book) or of one chapter (for, say, a middle-grade book), and make notes on the photocopies, crossing out words, replacing them and adding comments in the margins. This may sound almost sacrilegious but, hey, the author won't know.

Next step

It's now time to look at the wider world of writing: the next chapter discusses agents, publishers, writing groups and other opportunities out there for aspiring authors.

14

Beyond the book

In order to become a published author, you need to create work worth publishing. I hope that you have found plenty here to help you create that work. I hope, too, that you have started to develop your imaginative muscles and have seen a few purple horses along the way.

However, there is a great deal more to writing illustrated children's books than what is contained in these pages. Let's take a look at some of the options you can explore as you continue to develop as a writer of illustrated children's books: writing groups, writing courses, and conferences and festivals. This chapter also explains the different ways of publishing your book and the steps you need to take to get your book in front of the right people.

Creative writing groups

Writing is a lonely business. Unless you are inclined to the life of a hermit, there are times when you will be desperate to spend time with other people who understand the stresses and strains of what you are trying to achieve, and can act as an audience or a sounding board for your work. Look for creative writing groups in your area. Your local library will have information, as will the ever-ready Internet. Try to whittle it down to a children's writing group if you can, but a generic writers' group is a great place to start.

You could even start your own group. One of the many benefits of doing it this way is that you can dictate exactly what kind of group it is, when and where you should meet, and what type of biscuits need to be provided. Crucial stuff. You could even work your way through this book en masse. I'd love to know how that turns out.

Creative writing courses

Again, the Internet is a great source of information on creative writing courses if you want to really immerse yourself in the craft of writing for children. The best-known writing courses in the UK are run by the Arvon Foundation, who use published, often prize-winning authors to teach their courses: www.arvonfoundation.org. Many universities offer creative writing courses, too, with distance-learning opportunities available. You should perhaps bear in mind that doing a course like this doesn't guarantee publication at a later date, but it will give great, detailed grounding in all that writing and publishing entails.

Conferences and festivals

There seem to be more conferences and festivals celebrating children's writing with every passing year. In the UK, the Hay Festival is perhaps the best known, but there are also festivals in Cheltenham, Edinburgh, Bath and other cities that boast an extraordinary headcount of talented authors and illustrators happy to take the stage and share their secrets. You will meet like-minded people in the audience, in the beer tent and in the queue for coffee. Many festivals run workshops alongside the author and illustrator talks, which may give you further ideas on how to develop your writing.

Social media

Gone are the days when you had to write a letter full of breathless questions, then wait weeks in the hope that your literary hero would write back and share with you their secret of success. Many authors and illustrators spend their downtime these days on social media sites like Facebook and Twitter, where they are cheerfully available to the general public for questions and conversation in 140 characters or fewer – if your questions or conversation are interesting enough to catch their attention. Much can be gleaned about publishing life on these sites. There are often links to articles about writing and publishing, upcoming competitions, exciting book events and other relevant material. Even if you don't get a response from a favourite author, you are guaranteed to make lots of online writing friends by using hashtags such as #amwriting.

Literary consultancies

Literary consultancies provide a useful service to writers who want to polish their manuscripts before sending them to agents and publishers. They will go through your work with a fine-toothed comb, making suggestions on how you might edit and improve your writing and how then to present it to publishers. Consultancies such as Cornerstones (www.cornerstones.co.uk) use published writers and experienced editors to offer this tailor-made advice.

If you go down this route, be prepared to change your manuscript as advised in order to find a publisher, and then find that the publisher is likely to change it all over again. The editing process can be a deeply personal one, and what works for one editor may not work for another. If you are prepared for this, then there is much to be learned from the experience.

Key idea

Be sure to use a reputable firm. Check their references; call them up. If they don't have a landline or a physical address that you can check, I would be wary of parting with my money.

Agents

As mentioned several times in the course of this book, approaching agents is a much better way in than approaching publishers direct. Agents will only take on material with genuine promise, potentially saving both pride and postage, and then do all the legwork by approaching and negotiating with publishers on the writer's behalf. Publishers are *always* more likely to consider material submitted by agents they trust than material that arrives unannounced.

Do your research. Check those bibles of the writing trade, the *Writers' & Artists' Yearbook* (in the UK) and *Writer's Market* (in the US) for names, addresses and specialisms of reputable agents. *Never* pay an agent to take on your work. Genuine agents do not take money upfront. A real agent takes a cut of your profits only when they sell your book to a publisher, never before. If you find an agent who gushes about your book and then mentions payment for their services, block your ears to the flattery and run. Your book will never see the light of day.

Traditional publishers

If you are determined to take the direct route to a publisher regardless of the advice above, good luck. Again, use the *Writers' & Artists' Yearbook* / *Writer's Market* to give you names, addresses and specialisms. Don't make the rookie error of sending your illustrated children's poems to a publisher of non-fiction or war memoirs: it only wastes everyone's time.

The rule that applies to agents also applies to traditional publishers. If they ask for money upfront, they are not a traditional publisher. Traditional publishers generate their profits *after* your book has been published, and do all the marketing, publicity and distribution on your behalf. They offer writers an advance set against royalties. If your book sells well, you earn royalties over and above the advance you have already been paid. If your book doesn't sell at all, you don't have to return the advance. Phew.

How to approach an agent/ publisher

PRESENTATION

Firstly, ensure that your manuscript is meticulously presented. This means typed in a legible font on one side of A4 paper, with double spacing between the lines. It's a good idea to put your name and page number on each page as well, in case the pages ever get jumbled up or separated from one another. There should be no spelling or grammar inaccuracies.

If you are sending a picture-book text, try to break it down into the 32-page layout discussed earlier in this book. If you are unsure about how this layout works, simply write your text out word for word. A picture-book text shouldn't stretch to more than four pages of A4 paper, if you have limited your word count to a picture-book maximum of 1,000 words.

Key idea

Do not send pictures. They won't count towards the success or failure of your text, which has to be strong enough to work entirely by itself.

If you are submitting anything longer than 3,000 words, submit a one-page outline covering the main aspects of your plot and a maximum three chapters of text. Don't limit these chapters to your 'best bits' taken out of context; the whole manuscript should be strong enough to withstand scrutiny from page one. The book title can be as large and frilly as you wish, but the rest of the text must be strictly neutral.

COVERING LETTER

Now write a good letter to go with your manuscript.

A good letter isn't a long letter. A good letter is quite the opposite. A good letter is rarely longer than one page, double-spaced and neatly typed in a legible font. It should contain a brief introduction covering style/age range/word count for your book, a short paragraph summarizing the book (remember the work we did on blurbs and elevator pitches? – this is where those become invaluable), and a short paragraph about yourself if what you do is relevant to your approach. You should then sign off as politely and un-pushily as you can.

If you have researched other books that the agent/publisher represents, drop them casually into the conversation ('As you represent/publish Jacqueline Wilson, I wonder if you would be interested in representing/publishing my book, a contemporary story about a children's home') to prove that you have put in the legwork.

Only when your letter is as polished as your book – take extra care when checking for spelling and grammatical errors, which will instantly relegate you and your story to the recycling bin – should you put it in an envelope along with a copy of the manuscript (*never* the original) and, for extra Brownie points, a stamped addressed envelope for your manuscript's return.

Many agents and publishers now have an online process instead of a paper-and-ink approach. Literary agency Curtis Brown's www.curtisbrowncreative.co.uk/submissions is one example of this. It is cheaper and quicker and worth doing if the option is there.

Then be prepared to wait. It can take six weeks or more for a response. Don't chase for at least three weeks. It will feel like the longest three weeks of your life, but resist the temptation to call. Agents and publishers are busy people.

Key idea

Agents are also people who depend on writers like you submitting work to them which they might then go on to represent, so they will contact you when they can. Publishers are less likely to respond to a direct approach. They prefer agents to do this part for them.

Be prepared for the realities of submitting work to agents and publishers. Expect to fail at least five times. More than that, and you might want to put that story away and start work on a new one.

Try to submit your manuscript to one agent/publisher at a time. You may feel that you're saving time and effort by mass-mailing, but in the glorious event of an agent taking an interest, they might be put out to discover you've sent your book to five other agents as well. It's also a little rude, as it suggests a one-size-fits-all approach. Take your time. Flatter the person you're approaching with some knowledge and understanding of their field: the books they publish, the names they represent. You should be playing the long game.

The following sample submission letter can apply to both publishers and agents. There are no frills. Don't stray from the point. Keep it all on one page. Spell everything correctly. Type it out. Then let your manuscript speak for itself.

[Your address]

[*The agent's/relevant editor's name, correctly spelled*]

[*The agent's/publisher's address*]

[Date]

Dear [*Insert name, correctly spelled*],

I wonder whether you would be interested in representing my book, *Ernie's Problem*. It is a humorous picture book of 400 words aimed at five- to seven-year-olds, in the style of [insert similar style here, perhaps someone represented by the agent/publisher you are approaching].

Ernie is an earthworm with a problem. He wants to line-dance, but with only one leg he is struggling with the routines. By teaming up with his best friend Boris, can he make it to the local line-dancing finals? Or will Boris give in to temptation and take a trip to his team's football final instead?

I am [*a keen horticulturalist/botanist/line-dancing champion*] and [*insert anything relevant here e.g. other books you have written, artwork you have had published in magazines*].

I look forward to hearing from you.

Yours sincerely,

[*Your signature and name*]

Self-publishing

It's rare to find self-published books in illustrated fiction. It seems to be a genre that suits adult fiction better. Self-publishing is much more widely accepted these days than it used to be, but it's still a difficult road to success. If you take the self-published route, you have to pay your own way. You pay for editorial services, design, printing and distribution. The pay-off is a bigger cut of the profits, should any be generated, because you don't have any middlemen to deal with.

The benefits are there – ask E. L. James, self-published author of *Fifty Shades of Grey* – but you have to work hard for them because the onus is all on you. I liken self-publishing to an artist drawing a picture of a cat, hanging it on their sitting-room wall and hoping the world will drop by. It might be a great picture of a cat but, if no one knows it's there, what's the point?

Traditional publishing is more likely to get your cat into a public gallery, where more people will see it and, with luck, want to buy it. If you have the discipline, energy and cash to promote yourself via self-publishing, the world might indeed come to you – but it's extremely hard work, and not for the faint-hearted. If you just want to see your name in print and aren't worried about generating huge sales, then self-publishing may be a good route for you.

Online publishing

The world of online publishing has exploded in the past decade. Many online sites allow you to post stories for free, offer opportunities for feedback from fellow writers, help you generate new ideas and keep going with old ones. Groups such as The Writers' Workshop, Write Words and UK Authors are full of writers as keen on the idea of publication as you are.

The golden rule in the writing community is to be open to conversations with your readers. If you post stories and expect people to comment, you must return the favour and read and comment on other people's work in return.

Finishing work

It is hard to let go of something you have spent a long time creating. Hanya Yanagihara, author of *A Little Life* (shortlisted for the Booker Prize in 2015), confessed that she used to return home most days and create new scenes for characters who had, technically, flown the nest. The book stands at over 700 pages, but one gets the feeling it could have run and run if the author had had her time again. How do you let go? And then, when you have let go, how do you muster the energy to start again from scratch?

> ## Key idea
>
> Put on the kettle, have a biscuit, take a walk. Wallow in the void, daydream, doodle, fill the notebook with half-formed conversations, glimpsed expressions – and before you know it, you will have started the process all over again.

There is nothing better to take your mind off Project A than to embark on Project B. Writing and illustrating for children are all about practice. Each time you complete a piece of work, you are one step closer to realizing your dream of publication.

It's a slow business, but each step along the way yields rewards. Perhaps your first piece will never see the light of day. Maybe you will feel confident enough to send out your fifth piece of work to an agent; perhaps your fifteenth will get an encouraging response; perhaps, before you reach your twentieth, you will hear those magical words: 'I would like to represent/publish your book *Ernie's Problem*'.

I wish you the very best of luck on your journey. And I promise to buy the pencil.

Index